Hidden Water

A girl was in a wheelchair on her porch
And wasps were swarming in the cornice

She had just washed her hair
When she took it down she combed it

She could see
Just like I could

The one star under the rafter
Quivering like a knife in the creek

She was thin
And she made me think

Of music singing to itself
Like someone putting a dulcimer in a case

And walking off with a stranger
To lie down and drink in the dark

HIDDEN
WATER
From the
Frank Stanford
Archives

HIDDEN WATER

From the Frank Stanford Archives

Books by Frank Stanford

What About This: Collected Poems of Frank Stanford (2015)

The Light the Dead See: Selected Poems of Frank Stanford (1991)

Conditions Uncertain and Likely to Pass Away (1991; 2010)

You (1979; 2008)

Crib Death (1978)

The Battlefield Where the Moon Says I Love You: A Poem (1977; 2000)

Constant Stranger (1976)

Arkansas Bench Stone (1975)

Field Talk (1975)

Shade (1975)

Ladies from Hell (1974)

The Singing Knives (1971; 1979)

HIDDEN WATER

From the Frank Stanford Archives

Edited by Michael Wiegers and Chet Weise

Third Man Books
Nashville, Tennessee

TO ACCESS AUDIO:
http://thirdmanrecords.com/StanfordHiddenWater
password: FrancisGildart

 For information: Third Man Books, LLC, 623 7th Ave S, Nashville, Tennessee 37203.

Printed in Nashville, Tennessee

Library of Congress Control Number: 2015941268

FIRST EDITION
Cover design by Trent Thibodeaux. Book design by Nathanio Strimpopulos.
ISBN 978-0-9913361-3-5

About the cover: Frank Stanford asked his wife, artist Ginny Stanford, to paint his portrait with a black panther echoing Henri Rousseau's *The Sleeping Gypsy*. Stanford titled the portrait *Loss of the Killing Instinct*. The book cover is a black and white of the acrylic painting.

Table Of Contents

My wallet was thick as the bible I carried around
Graphs of Elvis Presley John Lee Hooker Briget Bardot and the sodbuster
I thought up non-de-plumeŝ in the outhouse and sent off Burns
for things cyptic ads I used stmps that made the postmaster
ask where I was from

Preface

I imagine that Frank Stanford would be somewhat bemused, and thoroughly gratified, at the sight of his manuscripts, drafts, business cards, letters, notebooks—his almost hormonal literary excesses, populated with gars, boats, cottonmouths, horses, and that ubiquitous moon—being perused by scholars and editors in an Ivy League reading room, preserved alongside centuries-old vellum-bound books, Latin hymnals, and illustrated maps, all under the watchful gazes of Gertrude Stein as painted by Dora Maar and by Francis Picabia.

While compiling and editing *What About This: The Collected Poems of Frank Stanford*, I made a few visits to the Beinecke Rare Book and Manuscript Library at Yale University. On the first of these trips I was joined by Chet Weise, who was helping launch a poetry line for Third Man Books—and was an admirer of Frank Stanford's poetry.

From the start of my editorial work on a "collected" Frank Stanford, I sensed that Stanford's poems, his biography, his legacy, the way he thought and composed—the entire endeavor—were ungovernable, almost beyond the scope of the single volume that would eventually become *What About This*. As pages from its working manuscript were increasingly filling my computer files, tabletops, and floors, I worried that a single Stanford retrospective would become too unwieldy, and so I focused on wrestling it into an agreeable order. When I was deep into the editing of the book, two things happened that made a second book feasible: Chet approached me with the idea of a collaboration between Third Man and Copper Canyon Press, and Ginny Stanford made available to Beinecke the remaining sizable portion of Stanford's archives.

What we had envisioned as a deluxe, enlarged edition of *What About This* quickly became its own stand-alone book—a collection of outtakes, original manuscript pages, letters, photos, and ephemera—which would communicate a fraction of the material we were encountering in the archives. As we fielded ideas—Chet suggested the title *Hidden Water*—our enthusiasm for this second volume grew. We traded our favorite discoveries and advocated for particular poems or images as together we further wrestled ungovernability. While emphasizing unpublished writing, we deliberately duplicated a small handful of poems across both books, in order to show the full sweep of his achievement.

The initial visit Chet and I made to Beinecke was a day spent opening folder after folder while the generous and patient Beinecke librarians brought to us carton after carton, as well as photo-filled flash drives. Certainly other researchers, poring over their equally enthralling texts, could hear our gasps—and a few Holy shit!s—as our surprise and enthusiasm grew in that otherwise bone-quiet room. In editing this book, the intent has been to convey our sense of excited uncertainty and wonder as we explored his papers, and to present the raucous energy we were encountering in that important treasure box of a library.

Maybe Stanford's "project" was never meant for completion. He wrote, rewrote, and repeated, often borrowing and stealing from himself, moving words around the page and layering them the way a painter moves paint. There is a manic, unstoppable energy to Stanford's work—and a predilection for a naked rawness in subject matter. Given his ever-shifting work habits, we often could not determine whether he had "finished" a poem. Lacking his imprimatur, we opted to foster a hint of incompleteness, presenting much of the work in facsimile—including pieces that were very much in flux, maybe even (temporarily?) abandoned.

We owe immeasurable gratitude to the librarians at the Beinecke and to Ginny

Stanford and C.D. Wright. Chet and I consider ourselves incredibly fortunate for having been entrusted with gathering together and stewarding this book.

There are many elements that call readers to the poetry of Frank Stanford: his preternatural facility with image and line, his humor, his passion for justice, his feral drive to be a part of the tradition of making. The amount of work he composed is breathtaking, for anyone at any age. Even his failures hold jaw-dropping lines. That moon, his pillow, those dreams, a flood.

— Michael Wiegers, 2015

Frank Stanford (1948-1978): An Appreciation

Frank Stanford, the poet, is the only man of whom I can say that I saw the movie and read the book before I met him. The movie was a film profile entitled *It Wasn't A Dream, It Was a Flood* in which a camera followed him around in Arkansas shadows. The book was his first volume of poetry, *The Singing Knives*, one of the most savagely beautiful books I know. Acquainted with him for just over a year, I felt I had never stopped seeing the movie, reading the book. He was that kind of figure, one you would scarcely expect to encounter outside works of the imagination.

"The work I do is not easy, / but it is not bad."

When I met Frank, he was a land surveyor, his profession of many years. Although my experience of land surveying begins and ends with *Kafka's Castle*, I thought Frank looked the way a land surveyor should. Or rather a surveyor out of a tale about a surveyor. He was physically imposing, built for subduing intransigent back country into a parceled obedience. His face was full of contrasts. Brutally handsome and fond of violent landscapes, it could bushwack you at odd moments with tenderness. His large eyes, often impenetrable, sometimes opaque with the aid of dark glasses, could be soft to the point of bovine, at rest after gazing at impossible distances. To see him was to be curious about what he'd seen. In his fur cap and tartan shirt he was a reassuring presence, and could make a refuge of a room. With him you might feel, when he relaxed his intensity, that you'd both just emerged from a storm.

But I had seen the movie, read the book, so I was wise to him. I knew he was masquerading, the way an explorer might pretend to be a pilgrim. And I knew the land under Frank's surveillance could not be reached by any charted route, that it was only accessible by following the map of his poems.

Though I considered him my friend, I didn't know him well. I had too much awe and envy for the legend to relate without pretense to the man. He spoke to me mostly of books that had moved him, treating their authors with comradely affection, as if he regularly visited them in the Underworld. He spoke also of his hopes for the press which has become his legacy; seldom of himself. Even now I know little of his past beyond the hearsay that preceded my meeting him, and much of that sounded like some hybrid tale of E.T.A. Hoffman upon Mark Twain. It is rumored, for instance, that Frank was an orphan who never knew his father, that he grew up in levee camps along the Mississippi, that he was treated for illness by voodoo herbalists and educated by monks, that he was a formidable exponent of the martial arts, that he wrote poetry from the time he learned to write words, wrote an 800-page verse narrative in adolescence, went to New York and returned an amnesiac, lived a recluse in the Arkansas woods and later with a wife who was an artist and beautiful, that he pulled the trigger three times when he came to take his life.

As a grownup I'd thought myself immune to such extravagance, but I wasn't. And in the end I suspect this: that the authentic history of Frank Stanford is wilder and more improbable than this sampling of rumors. It's a large pill to swallow. Who even daydreams with such romantic excess anymore? Makes you want to play down the facts of his life, like a scandal, lest they distort the issue of his art. But I don't think Frank's personal lexicon allowed for such a distinction. For it was the simple prodigy of his nature that his world and his imagination were identical. The visionary landscapes were the same ones he measured with his rods and theodolite; just as there was no discrepancy between the tract of universe on which he lived and the page on which he wrote. If I seem to suggest that he never quite fell from grace, so be it; surely that must be someone's definition of genius. As an orphan, he must have conceived his own heritage, woven himself a highwayman's cloak of mystery and fable. It was strange to meet the man wearing the same cloak, as if he'd forgotten to take it off; and the wonder was, it still fit.

This is not to imply that Frank Stanford's biography was nearly his best conception; its effects are too sensational. But certainly it deserves consideration within the body of his work.

To my mind the task of the surveyor was commensurate with the task of the poet. Both jobs involved traveling to a wilderness to mark boundaries and impose a tenuous order. This is how I presume he discovered and claimed for his own the very remote country of his poems—think of a spiritual Yoknapatawpha. "My poetry is no longer on a journey," he said before his death, "it has arrived in its place." How far he traveled to find his province I can only guess. To record such distances requires a surveyor's skills and instruments capable of measuring the miles between daylight and dreams.

Thus, to see Frank in the streets of Fayetteville, where I knew him, was like meeting Marco Polo back from Cathay. Whenever our paths crossed, he would shake my hand heartily, as if pleased he was still recognizable. Because Frank had become a citizen of the country to which he'd journeyed—in town he was a foreigner, the constant stranger from the title of one of his last books. So deep was his pleasure in stories and films, in good whiskey and jazz, headlines, snowfall, the clothes a woman was wearing, that you had the impression the ordinary world was his retreat. He might have been eavesdropping on an exotic culture. You felt he'd been away a long time and was imminently leaving again—not that he ever seemed in a hurry. "The hours in ambush like medicine in a dark bottle," he wrote; but I had the impression Frank took his medicine only when it pleased him to cure himself temporarily of wandering. Time, for the surveyor, was only another boundary subject to his own calculations.

His personality was a magnet for outcasts and misfits of every persuasion, who presented themselves like volunteers for the population of his poems. Poor blacks, threadbare poets, genuine outlaws, maverick women—assembled, they might have been passengers on an immigrant ship bound for a port in a dream. You felt select in such company, as if the ship were an ark and the world in floodtime. With women Frank had a special rapport, which I believe was connected to his peculiar dialogue with the moon. The moon was Frank's familiar. Throughout his poems he personified and disguised it, producing it from out of pockets and under hats. "The moon went back into its night / Like a blue channel cat in a log."

"I suppose that at one time there was a ship. . . / and it had a great cargo, the moon"

"The moon wanders through my barn / Like a widow heading for the county seat"

"A woman bootlegger shook her dustmop / That was the moon."

Of course Frank's character in its heroic mold would have drawn women to him anyway. But I always fancied that women who knew him well shared with him a secret, as if the moon were a child or a talisman he'd placed in their safekeeping.

He liked to give gifts, in keeping with his image of a wayfarer returned from foreign parts. There was always ceremony in their presentation, the gifts like trophies commemorating an adventure. Once he gave me a book of poems bearing the cryptic inscription: "Does this cat have nine lives?" It was his ninth book of published verse. Another time he gave me the manuscript of a poem entitled "You." He handed it to me furtively and peered over my shoulder as I read it, as if it were a message he'd found in a bottle.

Late of an evening I've heard Frank, grown restless, say to a roomful of friends, "Let's put on a pot of coffee and write all night." Who else would have suggested this sort of literary quilting bee? He had a talent for exasperation, might try to infect you with enthusiasms you'd rather not contract, tell you the ends of movies you'd yet to see. And when you were feeling cozy in the seclusion of your labors, he might try to instill in you some sense of a grand collaboration. "Put on an overcoat," he might as well have said, "and let's travel all night." Writing is a journey, it was that simple. We could all depart jointly, progressing at our own respective speeds, and still arrive at the same place by morning. It was to that place—which few of us could have reached on our own steam—that Frank wanted to take us. We resisted of course, fidgetting and offering excuses, and later on regretted that we'd been left behind.

He pressed his poems on us like snapshots of an unnamed country. "A swatch / of her daughter's nightgown / fluttering on the barbed-wire," "one star under the rafter / quivering like a knife in the creek," "a young man, blind from birth, suddenly closing an accordian," "the gravesites of stars," "a cemetery of dreams"—these were some of the features of that country. They were photographs of hallucinations which, conjured into existence, seemed always to have been, and we recognized them as the longlost fragments of our memories. Frank never seemed to have anything particular to prove. Yet he showed us his poems as a kind of evidence, as if, on some ordinate survey of Arkansas or the soul, he'd located a spot equidistant from heaven and hell.

When I knew him in Fayetteville, he seemed to be tarrying, to have relaxed for a spell the arduous myth he was living. Occasionally you felt he was not above receiving a laurel or two, accepting the measure of lionization that was his for the taking. But Fayetteville is a university town, where the curriculum can sometimes include the clinical leaching of myths. There were those unacquainted with his credentials who could dismiss his ingenuousness as pose. So you worried that Frank had made himself vulnerable. You thought that, apart from the threat of self-consciousness, a myth is most in peril when least believed in. If you were a friend, you feared that, should Frank stay too long away from his wilderness, he might lose his way back again. (The name of his press, established in Fayetteville, is incidentally called Lost Roads.) Could be that anxiety was wasted on Frank, whose vision comprised a portable atmosphere, but you worried nonetheless and tended to view his premature end as justification for that worry.

His stories and poems are full of marvelous children. They speak with their hands, live with solitary women, stand against the wall of an outhouse while knives with names are hurled at them. In forests, ruined steamboats, nightmare hotels, they spy upon fearful truths and take illicit draughts of wonder. They are incorrigible. Accosted by the Angel of Death, they face him down with a swaggering disrespect.

"I said I was a orphan. / See these suspenders? / They hold up my pants. / I sleep where I please, / My pillows are from the best roosters." They are the Our Gang of Frank's imagination, playmates invented in childhood whose company he never left. Where they're involved in his writing, his writing is a game of inspired mischief. Much of the edifice of his art has in fact been vandalized by the scuff-marks and graffiti of these children.

"Children trying on gloves. Children in the gardens of their retinas. . . / Children. . . like ships running guns. / Held to the veranda by a ghost and blackbird pie, / Held to the dark by invisible binoculars. Children / in the garden of the moon. . . ." There was no corridor or room in his poetry too sacred to play in. A fool for irreverence, Frank burlesqued his own memento mori, mocked his own manhood by never quite growing up.

So it was a contraband thing, his innocence, smuggled intact out of childhood. (There are poems in his early collections dating from 1957, when Frank was preposterously nine years old.) His attitude toward his prodigious gift was like a smuggler's toward his booty. As a kid his delinquency must have had a literary bent, which involved the pillaging of books and the rifling of their contents.

"There are bookshelves I threw together / I took the lumber / From a horse thief's barn / And there are books the dead light their stoves with / Books howling like pines on a ridge / Cats in heat / Deserted and cold like a handgun or a spoor / A gar looking for a wife in a swamp. . ." I see him on a rampage, abetted by his imaginary lieutenants—Jimmy and Willow, Hushpuckena, Born-in-the-Camp-with-Six Toes—robbing the graves of Lorca and Cocteau, stealing tchatchkes from Prospero's Cell. Then he flees with his loot straight through the customhouse of adolescence, where most of us declare almost everything. Proud of his spoils he showed them off. "I don't want my work to be vague or obscure," he said. "I want to show the origins." So he would take from his sack a few relics—a bagpipe, a bird's split-tongue, a hat of smudge candles, Cocteau's dandruff—meaning to expose the mechanisms of illusion. Then he, the thief, was as surprised as we were to find that the sack contained vintage magic.

In the landscape of his poems it is nearly always twilight or dark.

"I open the doors of my house at night."

I don't know when he began to build his house, but I can picture him breaking ground at dusk, emptying his box of tools, his sack of spoils. Then, like a kid building a clubhouse with odds and ends, with scraps of floating hair and the hundred personae of the moon, he commences to hammer and saw. The result is a kind of architectural folly, haunted by nearly everything. It is full of eccentricities:

"A door leading to a cemetery, a library of dreams. / Rooms and rooms of crumbs and starlight, / Drawers hard to loosen but filled with shoelaces and dark glasses, / Bibles thick as pigmeat." There are mirrors; but whereas most poets work on one side of the looking-glass indicating the other, in Frank's house a mirror is just another threshold.

Once I compared Frank's labors (immoderately) to the ancient Britons, who quarried their magic blue stones in Wales and dragged them, by dint of divine strength or madness, across England to Stonehenge. Later I took it all back. Words and stones lose their holiness when removed from their original context; Stonehenge has degenerated into another roadside attraction. But Frank kept his stash of icons and images close to their native soil, installed in poems like enchanted museums. To see them you cross boundaries into a humid and dangerous zone, you enter his house.

Sometimes I've made the mistake of trying to take up residence in words. Invariably I suffocate. Few books have a climate that can support human life for long; few books have windows. Most authors, as if they believed that the book contains the world, simply neglect to put them in. I've said that through some blessing or psychic flaw Frank seemed to make no distinction between the book and the world. A practical visionary, he built structures for people to live in. Often I make the retreat into his works. They're an unlikely place to seek sanctuary, neither comfortable nor secure. The situation is treacherous, the house gothic and crazy, its windows open in all weather. But if the wind blows wildly through its rooms and passages, through our bones, at least we don't forget we're alive.

"I have seen doors / through which death comes and goes," he wrote, speaking of the entrances to an annex he'd built onto his abode. It was a wing to which you gained access by crossing another boundary Frank never recognized.

"In these rooms death grows / On the shady side of the mountains like ferns / And that isn't right either / Because death is also sagegrass, belladonna, and rosehips. . ."

The German novelist Heinrich Boll said somewhere that an artist should carry his death like a priest his breviary. If so, then Frank had his hymns to death at matins, at vespers, had them for a lullabye. I think he meant to spellbind death with his singing. In this he was still the child, curious rather than morbid, meaning to fascinate the beast in order to become intimate with its mystery. It is the same audacious impulse that incites a boy to prowl about a derelict mansion or steal upon a girlfriend's clothesline.

"When no one is looking / We touch the thin underthings / Of our death to our lips."

In his poetry Frank Stanford travelled back and forth between life and death as if passing from one room to another. Two decades ago he went into one of the farthest rooms and locked the door behind him. This is not to say he abandoned the house.

— Steve Stern, 1978
Asheville Review (revision, 2000)

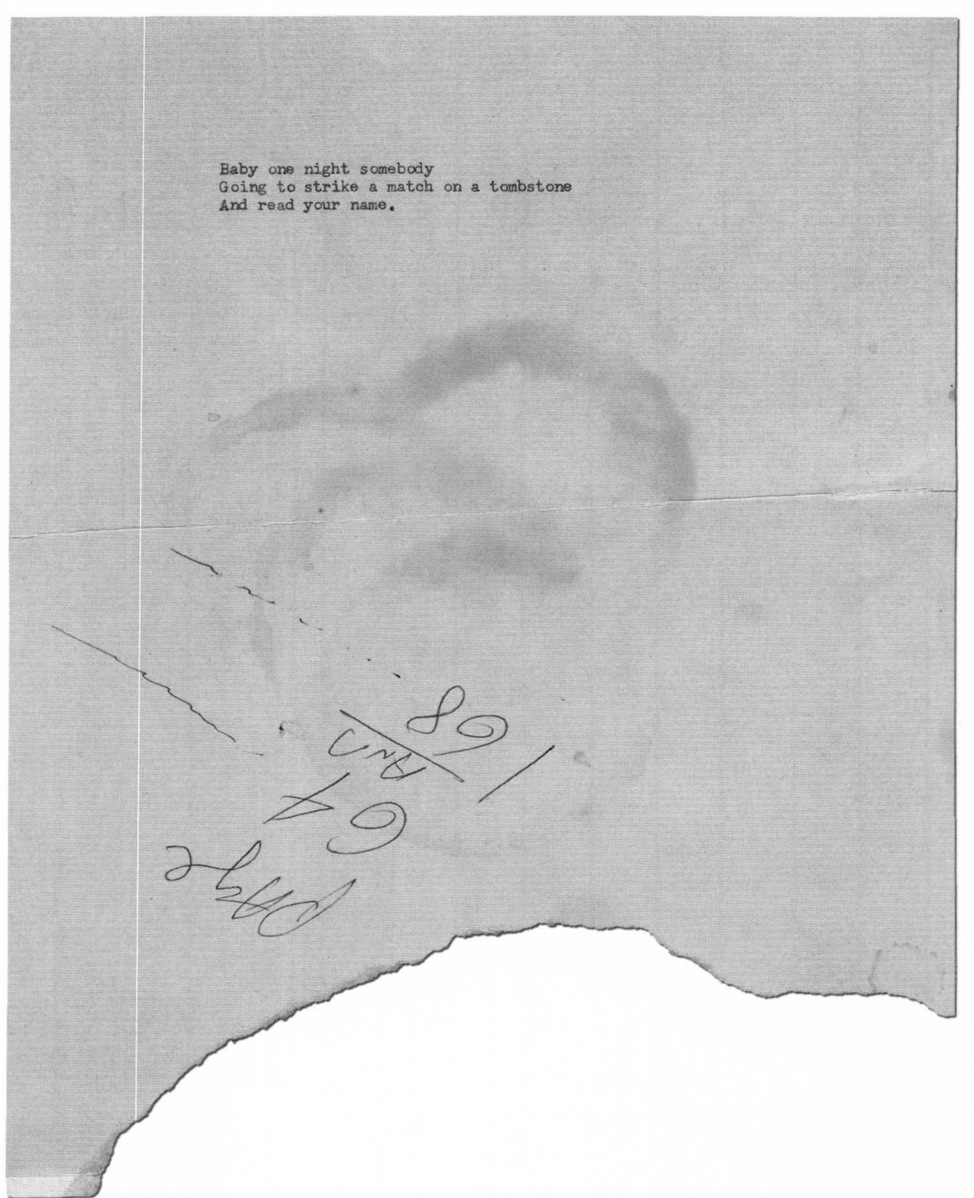

Baby one night somebody
Going to strike a match on a tombstone
And read your name.

I. The Mind Reader and Other Poems

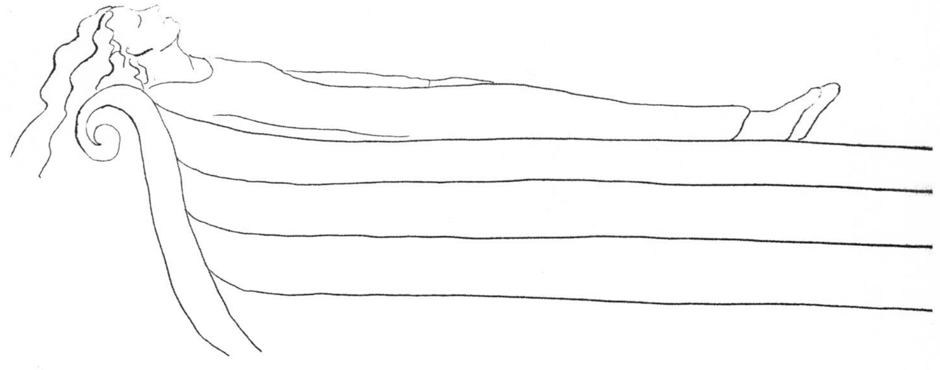

The Moon

I think it is a ship
    putting out without me
A white horse
    that throws all riders
And a swimmer who is naked
    who believes she is asleep
It is a rooster
    molting dark feathers in the water
Or a beekeeper who dreams
    someone has found her out in the garden
A snake which sheds
    its skin in the riverbed at night
And a schoolgirl weeping
    under a black patch
I know it is only a stone
    everybody keeps a blind date with

the song keeps running off
it is like a wild pony
now where did it go to this time
my blood walks down the road like a drunk man
I look for it in the clouds the fresh pillow cases
I see the carriage
carrying the dead ballerinas into the wilderness
the passengers with wet slippers
and the ship bearing the harpsichord of dead lovers
is putting out like a smoldering pyre
I walk along the docks
I call for the son I won't put a bit in its mouth
when it's dark
the hunter goes off into the mountains
I hear his truck and I see the lights
but there aren't any mountains we both know that
I am the prey of night and she is always
stalking me she puts the doubloons over my eyes
I dream about robbers
and children rising up like vines around the eaves
all clasp hands we swim in the rivers
we cut our palms open with butcher knives
and grip one another
the blood brothers and sisters of each land
I dream of wide-eyed babies in jars of formaldehyde
I dream of submarines
and men suffocating in their own blood
I dream of the filthy moon
where the rifles are stacked like the harvest is over
the riverboat men boiling crawdads in the shanties
and I dream about mermaids' hair
there are women driving Cadillacs to Memphis at tremendous speeds
my dog died a long time ago
look at the teeth of the piano on the highway
there's no money under my pillow
only the unwinding rope in the fathoms of sleep where I give my only commands
to the water
I strut around with my hands over my mouth
two ribbons tickle the back of my neck
the rooster floated down the river on a ladder the men are standing in the boat
with the oars upright
I am the sentry of my dreams
I ride a black horse
I am blind and a swordsman of some rank
when you see the coffin ship you see me dead ahead
I am the acolyte of the forest

in the evening you can hear me crossing the bridge
I put a blessed rosary on my trout line
I say my hail marys to the gars
my friend is the trespassing dog
in the country where pistols are kept like photographs
I am the target I am the album
I run with convicts and gypsies
I dream I yell on the mountains
a pair of black boots
ride upside down in the stirrups
I was washing off the wound
I was throwing the knife
I was lying under the switchwillow tree
I was eating cherries
the pig was sucking my toe
I had a notion it might rain while the pirate cried
I can tell things like that
I can read minds
robbers and cottonmouths don't bother me
I make fun of the devil
I take the angels fishing
I sing in the woods
I sing to mother so I can sing
I sing to the creek
I dream so I can dream so I can pee in the Mississippi River
so I can bless the sailors
I dream about milk I dream about rifles
I dream about stamps like jungles I dream about the operas mother plays
I dream about keels
I dream about the midget who stole my boots off the bridge while I was
swimming at night
I dream-kiss my foot
I dream about old songs and my dreams sing back to me
I dream about a Negro sewing canvas
my dreams are like turtles they never let go
they are thunder and lightning
I keep a night watch over the territory of my bed
I whistle in my sleep to the mares
they cave in the levee sure enough the night is dark
they ride into the lobby like General Forrest he lied
my dreams are like ticks they suck that blood
I get sick in the early hours
sometimes they make me cry
sometimes I feel like a motherless child
I smile at my enemies the sad javelins no one will throw
I feel sorry for the devil he was an angel
my dreams make me kiss my tears underground
they make hind tracks full of blood
they play a guitar with a dead man's knife

they have teeth like a gar they make me say excommunicated tambourine
at the spur of the moment
they make me train with my Sensei to fight like Bujin
to be silent
and learn the torsion of the hand the tiger mouth and my throws
are like going over a waterfall in a dream
a bear paw for the throat a knife hand for the ribs
a tiger gnawing its foot
for the belly an iron horse against more than three
a spirit like the moon a mind like the water
the gentle way of empty hands
I am the samurai kneeling beside the still water
my battles are all over
I bow to them and they bow to me the honorable lost ritual the memory
I get up at dawn and meditate
I breathe
I swim the channels alone
I fight against the knife and sword
I fight against the ones older and larger than myself
sometimes I get knocked out
my favorite strangle is the Hadakajime the naked choke
my favorite throw is Ukigoshi the floating hip
I'm built for Haraigoshi the sweeping loin
I dream about Japanese warriors
I dream about the blind koto players
I dream about the great swordsmen doing battle
my sleep is a chauffeur
my bed is a hearse driven by its passenger a drunken gypsy
my room is a back road of white dust you have never passed over
in my dreams I go anywhere
the teams of mules have no eyes
I know the songs of the jive cat Charlie B. Lemon
I am a personal friend of his
my dreams sing in the choir like him
they pitch curve balls for WDIA like him
they drive the Cadillac like him
they use a ice pick with a high yellow
they use good-time dust like monkey women
my dreams make me crazy
they are like drowned schoolgirls who hold my hand in the moonlight
I fall in love right off the bat
do you see virgins riding bareback
I have eleven girlfriends
every night I dream I am a seafarer in a ship with one of them
I pretend I kiss the pillow
I am always by myself
sometimes I walk up to people and knock the daylights out of them
I stare at the ladies at the picture show
in the restaurants I look at them

and I tell my mother isn't that lady beautiful
my mother was beautiful I've seen pictures
sometimes I'm a gentleman
I walk downtown with a tweed suit on
and tip my cap to the ladies like Errol Flynn
my father seldom speaks
when he does everyone hushes he's the boss
I go to sea in my dreams I go to hell in my dreams
they are sweet as sweet can be they are as strong as coffee
my dreams howl at the moon
my dreams are like sagas like Viking ships
I dream about bears in Snow Lake
I dream about beautiful wolves nobody sees but me
I dream about dogfights
I dream about traps
I dream about helping convicts make a break
I did it
I dream about the death of Rob Roy was eleven rivers of blood
I dream about peckerwoods turning folks in
they sell them down the river
I dream about scalawags and their suitcases of lies and friends
I dream about politicians with beeshit in their teeth
just look at them paying off their henchmen the trash
I dream about the good outlaws coming back one day
and running the cowards out of town
I dream black hands and white hands like where two creeks meet
I dream about prisoners strangling guards with log chains
I dream about men singing with axes I dream the red heads rolling
blessed are the cripples they have to haul everybody's load
blessed are the ugly they will be beautiful in heaven
blessed are the mothers crying in the death bed alone their sons won't come home
blessed are the no counts because they may have had a hard time
blessed are the people who make it bad on others maybe they'll know one day
blessed are the innocent they never had a chance
blessed are the fish I hook in the mouth blessed are the worms
blessed are the one-eyed minnows blessed is unbound hair
blessed is Stonewall Jackson my daddy's daddy saw him fall off his horse
blessed is Abe Lincoln he was a good man I believe
blessed is Baby Gauge we were going to school in the field
blessed is the spotlighted deer taking two loads of double-ought buckshot
blessed are the chunks of lung leaving a trail
blessed are the composers nobody will listen to
blessed are the drunks I like to talk to them and the clouds
blessed is the bald-headed preacher shooting somebody in the ass on account
of his wife blessed is the one that got shot
blessed are the wild horses let them be wild forever so I can dream
so I can swim in the lagoon of shotguns so I can ride the black steed myself
so I can duck out of the way of the limbs so I can say goodnight so I can sing

about the last ship I dream about the last crew
the sleeping virgins in the forecastle the dreaming rudders in the sea
the folded arms of the lovers the ambrosia keel the waking girl
the fish blood in the trunk of the Buick the flies on the hood in the fall
the door tied on with dynamite wire where the buck charged him
the love letters I put in the whiskey bottles I put in the slough
weeping gypsy dressed in black galloping through the woods
did you see him I did
a guitar bleeding to death did you hear it I did
the black arrows shot by the falling horsemen did you feel them I did
the rendezvous of the telescope and the bullcalf was kept
the rendezvous of the keelhauled innocent was kept
everything is kept in the silence of bloody lips
the shark was kept married in the sea the truth was kept in a shut mouth
the ship was kept in the harbor but the knife wasn't kept in the scabbard
it has always been kept in the hearts of the holy the damned
it doesn't matter if I shut my eyes or open them I can always see
the dancing boots of sundown
the grave medallions what about the autographed baseballs
the sleepwalker's dream horse
the beat-up colored man
the pistol-whipped gravy
the Swede bleeding out of his ear
the Episcopalian ghost ship
the knife in front of him
the prayer O.Z. said when he buried Jimmy's wolf ashes to ashes dust to dust
the shallow water where the sun comes up and I am half asleep
a man with his thumbs in his suspenders
a woman lighting a wood stove
a man putting grease on his hair and eating cornbread
the high-English brush back and the do-rag Ray Baby can't untie
a dog coughing a fish bone out of his throat
a man drinking buttermilk with dried-up goose blood on his fingers
a jar of it on the porch
a woman with light skin wiping crumbs off her lips
the hunters starting up their trucks
the picture of me looking through a brown half-pint bottle Tangle Eye
threw in a ditch
a fish hook somebody is going to step on
the field hands rolling out of the bed of the pickup slow as sorghum
the lost hoe file
the revolver in the paper sack
already it was nighttime
a peckerwood cutting his daughter's hair in the outhouse with a pocketknife
a bloodstained pair of pants
one stinking toe-holed shoe
somebody cracking their knuckles

the fish scales on the plank looking like silver dollars
the hide on the barn
the firecrackers Melvin threw on the white preacher's church I got the whipping
the deathwatch over the cook and her grandpa was chief of the Creeks
that means she was a griffe
Emma is a sambo
the beanflip Baby Gauge shot the midget with
it will chuck a rock clean across the river
the blessing at sea of the blind warriors the Bushido
the corridors of Creole songs and crawdads one dollar a bucket
the hoodooqueen from New Orleans selling tobies and Mexican good-luck water
the frog gig he did himself
the castrated horses breaking wind
the thrown-out supper grease running down the bank
the young woman washing her tits in a red-rimmed dish
the flashlight I dropped off the bridge it burned all night
the time Jimmy let me watch him screw a girl
he showed me how to jack off
the gantry where they lynched a man they said he was a rapist
the knife thrower's wife was Italian she was naked
the bleeding roses the wagon wheel the burial vault in Verona
they won't believe me when I get back to Memphis I carved in the outhouse
the white suit with the ticket stubs of the last picture show I saw in the pocket
the magician threw his knife in a tree for a thousand years it rusts and the tree
grows around it I listen to it I don't have to think about it
the buried knife is the trumpet of the voyage of the wolf heart
the night bears its wound the tree bears its wound
the virgins bear their wounds the knife bears its wounds the ship bears a wound
and school starts tomorrow
there is pigshit under the house with the chickens and the geese
and the name of my school is Sherwood not the forest
they hung Robin Hood a long time ago
they burnt his bow up and the arrows turned into driftwood
they stuffed their pillows with the feathers
their bellies with poor folks' meat they turned the dogs
loose on my dreams
I can't be at peace anymore
Maid Marian she's a whore
and all the merry men shook hands and dropped dead
the sheriff's boys got them
so long Friar Tuck you pig pray for me
cut a fart when you lay the Host in the hangman's mouth
so long Baby Gauge
we'll never go to school together
keep a lookout on the levee
don't let Baby Ray drown keep the high sign for you know who
the school that shit hole

the sepulcher of report cards I got straight A's
I hate it
let all the children raise up in their dreams
let them all slit their wrists
let them swear their oaths in their sleep
and it will be known throughout the lands
we are the dream children
in the classrooms assault your teachers
they're so full of shit they don't
know it
everybody going around like blow flies
kissing each other's ass the leeches
phooey
I say goodbye to the rivers
goodbye
to the fields
goodbye to the earth where I can dig good bait
so long fish I'll get you next year
I see the teacher now with her shovel
in repose I'll wait in my grave
when boys are licking calumny's boots I depart
I say goodbye to those tongues
have mercy on them sweet Jesus if only they could dream
farewell sister with your black-eyed peas
so long Dark with French harp
I remember you in the dead of night
I can only say goodbye
take it easy friends don't let anybody mess with my hound
I want to strip down
I'll read the book I stole out of the library *The Virgin and The Gypsy*
so far doesn't make much sense it would in a boat though
I want to lay my head in my mammy's lap so long
I want these flies out of my sweetmilk
I want these teachers to let me go in peace
I am leaving take care of the deaf and dumb man
I want to sing
I dream about Greece about scimitars about arbalests about Mozart about Gulliver
the sword in the rock the lady in the lake the burning rope Gunga Din
the falcon and the hood
the Green Knight and the Black Knight
I swore an oath to the archangel to joust with evil all my life
the son in the moon the night the cup of blood
I dream
I make up ships I look up dresses I read plays I talk to myself
I am waiting to draw a ship that will carry me away
back to Sukey jump camp doing the old breakdown
make a B line to Elaine
a black ship with fine timber some of that good ash from over around Friars Point
a ship without a rotten plank

a ship where everyone will have his turn at the wheel
a ship where the incantation of oars is never heard
a ship where the only prayer is the wind and it says
what did I bring you not the savanna of fangs not the leagues of loneliness
I bear blessings boss I got it all the dancing captain says
I guide you through the sleeping rivers I keep the snakes out of your tent
I carry you through the songs of the graveyard
through the passages of lost swords
bless my soul
blessed ship bearing the wounds of the world
the ship of dreams sighted by blind riders
ship that puts out light and darkness
ship betrothed to the wilderness
a ship bearing the tortured corpses of the horses my friends you will be
healed by the constellations I make up so I can follow them so I can dream
black stallions wounded riders sleeping girls
black as the moon black as a paw black as Baby Gauge
I'll have such a crew in the gospel ship
me and my dreams
like Saint Francis and the wolf

Embark

a few years back there was a lamp
that shone on nothing
which was
my boat
the wick was so quiet you could hear it
like a thwart
of headfeathers so black
they are purple the favorite color of death
mother was kind and dark
my brother set the hook good
he saw the hunchback in the diving bell
we sung to the hypnotist and his stableboy
knowing full well we should have sang
I composed to the soft-shelled turtles without earrings
in other words
I reached down for delight
and I scattered
dust like circles you can't draw
I waited
for the black knight of the plow
to sound
like an auctioneer
who did chiropracting on the side
there were traces gouging me
and singletrees rubbing me out
I was known like a landing
where convicts ditched their clothes
where dead men floated home with fish on their lines
and their big toes cut to the bone
only mud and the small death of the wild card
just the saga of squeals
and the undecipherable rigors
of the bobcat at sundown
the termites' hieroglyphics
the temperatures of the body of a songbird
and the arcanum of thick lips and other strange domains
I put pollen on my toast
and dunked it in a shewolf's milk
I nursed the teat of sorrow made scarlet like a stranger
or something which shudders
each second turning over its spell
was a vignette giving alms to the nicked deer
a mammy a good hunching of blood
a climbable tree no one will swing from
and an odor
by the time it took a shadow to abandon a puddle

I had sketched out a scenario a streak of music with a crust
like a mouth you whittle out
of the air with your bad teeth
to kiss
when their time of the month does not come
and there are no home games left
and the fast girls of junior high are laying you low
I kneaded feathers and fishhooks
and got away with it
the early morning rain flushed the bees from my shirt
I was like a legend no one had got around to
hearing left my daddy like a mistress
who had quite a brood to look after
and I followed her with the moon on my thumb like a blister
I was not a gypsy but pretty near
like him
the word edifice was a strange rock
with something scribbled on the damp side
a mold standing you up at the dances
you're too poor to attend
anyhow
wherever I've forgotten the steps
of my departure
I'll remember the evening as a rebus
of fairly good times of suffering
without the hint of memory
after all is grace

The One-Eyed Tiger

eyebrow
singing under a cross of ashes

Cottonmouth

He blossoms
in a green creek
like a doe
flashing her flag
in the forest.

the dreams

I can dream in a boat
I can dream in a tree
I can dream riding a horse
I can dream in a ditch
I can dream eating strawberries
I can dream while I'm swimming
I can dream on a bulldozer
I can dream in the Peabody Hotel
I can dream in the outhouse
I can dream with the convicts working on the road
I can dream underwater
I can dream at the Malco
I can dream I'm drifting through the centuries in a black ship
I can dream my mother was a wolf
I can dream a man in a robe standing vigil over my grave
I can dream the swift steed of the gods
I can dream all the dead riders
I can dream watching the shooting stars in a black dog's eye
I can dream a piano of bourbon
I can dream on Beale
I can dream even though I am asleep in a star drift
I can dream about tides
I can dream about the spiral galaxies
I can dream my investiture of dreams
I can dream I'm the guest of my brother sleep
I can dream a sword of ice dipped in wine
I can dream I'm death ringing in your ears
I can dream a mast the blackest shadow of night
I can dream I've been building levees for fifty years like daddy
I can dream I'm a big shot on the river like him
I can dream I'm always silent like him
I can dream I'm a root picker like Tangle Eye
I can dream I'm a lost sailor
I can dream I awaken inside a viola de gamba
I can dream sometimes I'm a bee and sometimes a bear and my heart is a honeycomb
I can dream gun powder gives me a headache
I can dream cleaning grave mud off my boots with a knife
I can dream in Sho Nuff's tent when he makes the dynamite
I can dream mother is smiling in the house of fortune

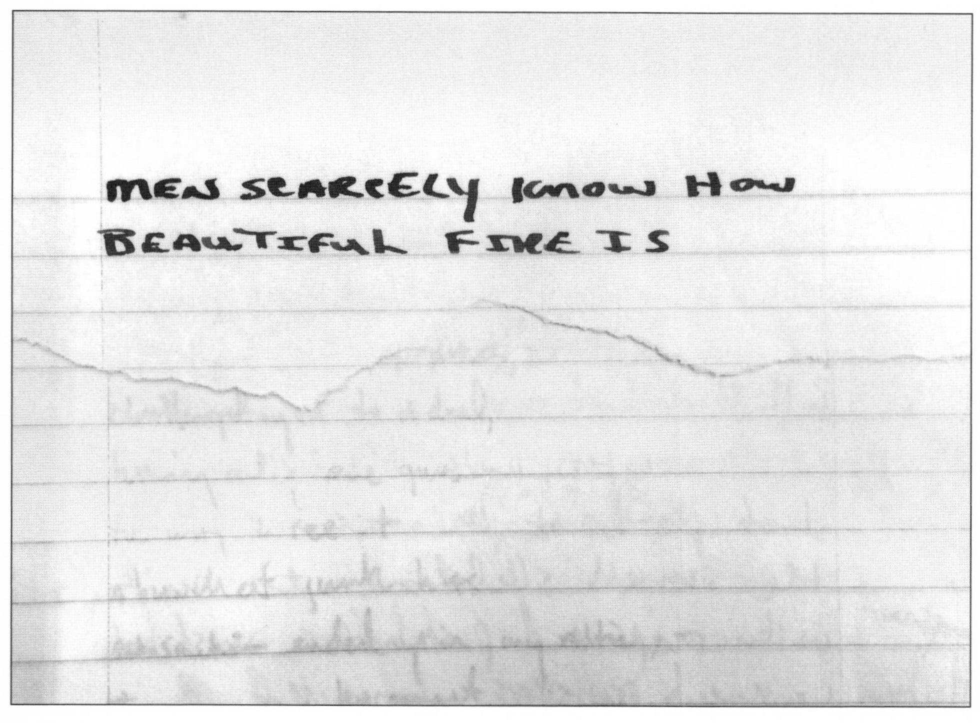
MEN SCARCELY KNOW HOW
BEAUTIFUL FIRE IS

barn dance

the clock struck something deep in the river
a boy and his grandpaw dreamed
the guitar was lampsmoke and no more
the sisters and daughters were lunar like kettles
filled with boiling hogs

they were grinning

marvel and grace and naked form
and proof of it besides

I threw a rock as soft as a throat
and something went out
a cloud
got in by mistake
the caller shut the door on it
they rolled it up like a parachute
and then they began to laugh
like death tried to boogie

the buckdancer went crazy in the loft
and straw floated in the cider
tools went into orbit
men threw away keys and talked
precisely as the foot of a rabbit

I might even say it got me nowhere
this was land
the cooks squinted in the early hours
things became sloped
no one noticed the hour

53

the shipwrecked dancers

the flashing eyes
and do you remember
the girl sang very well

The Night Ride

I road across the delta on the horse called blue
I was silence I know it like the back of my hand
the delta was a river without a boat
where death is in the ditches on the side of the road
there was a meeting on the levee
and a convict on a mule
there was clapping there was gunfire
and the moon was a colored man saying amen in a robe
I rode through the water I was
a song I know it

My Hands Were Warm

My hands were warm
In the slashed pockets

Now you are seeing it my way

So long Camille of the hills
And you dark things in the valleys
Where are you
Lips of the dry run
And eyes
Of the lightning before death
Let's ship out one of these nights
Then again goodbye
And yodel
Fucking it all away
Fucking it all away

II. Blue Yodels and Other Songs

I need copies of these poems, but you keep copies for yourself.

You know those series of old poems beginning 1957 through 1964, eight poems in each , 64 peoms in all; they begin 1957 SOME POEMS THAT WERE WRITTEN ON BARGE PLANKS, from PICTURE SHOE ON THE RIVER, THE NIGGER WHO DID IN THE DANCER, THE MOONCALF, poems are flake, driftwood, doom, grave, the coming of night, widow, nightingale, the negro child with the dipnet in one fist and the match in the other, all continuing through 1964. PLUS below:

BLUE YODEL THE MANY EVENINGS

THE NOCTURNAL SHIPS of the PAST

CREST PART III Some PAST TWELVE

H.D. who is drinking....

NAEGLING: Bequeath

Regret Des Yeux....

ST. FRANCIS AND THE WOLF:
baldachin
A stowaway on the ship of the past
organ
one-eyed tiger
wooden tower
I would have A woman AS real as death

Naegling: The LAST Dance after Jean Follain

ANCHORESS

The SECOND Night, VAlley, Amnesia,
Bearing in mind the past few days

BLUE YODEL Of The Closely Watched Bridges

Seven days ago they let Duquesne
Out of the penitentiary
He knows the truth
And they didn't get it
Or give him a fair trial
And so the men from town
Are watching the river right well
Wondering where Jean Duquesne will cross
They know he's bound to spend the first night
At Miss Heddy Grace's place
Then he'll go visit the good Brothers
At the Abbey of St. John of the Cross
The ones who talked the warden
Into an early parole
He'll confess take the sacraments and drink
With them
They'll give him a mule and their blessing
They know the river
Is too high to cross on the back
Of any animal
And he doesn't want to die bad
Enough to take a boat
So'll look for a bridge
But before he comes over any water
There are graves he has to visit
Graves not forgotten [illegible] never attended
While he's breaking
Dogwood branches to scatter
The men lying in wait
Near the bridges will turn
Up their collars blow on their hands
And bite their furred gloves
Keeping the trigger fingers warm
Day and night two old friends who've fallen out
Will pass by again without speaking
A guitar string breaks and no one
Mends it
Like a live oak growing around barbed wire
Nothing is stretched but bones
It rains five days and the clouds grow dark at night

The moon disappears
Like a plow
Losing its shine the wet men in ambush
Have forgotten those who remember
Jean Duquesne
There's Slow Joe Willett and his brothers
Gunnar Bull the one-legged Swede
And Father Mark Bavon
There are enough of them to cover every bridge
All his friends need is light
Or one of the others
Trying to strike a match in the rain

Blue Yodel of Those Who Were Always Telling Me

You look like you just woke up

What did you do last night
sleep in the fields

Now all of you who ride the schoolbus
during deer season   be sure
and duck down on the backroads

Get on out of here

Honey   Mama Julinda gone fix your eye

Sign my yearbook   Don't
write anything like you did in Beth's

You know you can't come in my theatre
unless you got shoes on

Bait my hook   that's what I'm paying you for

Why don't you go to Memphis
and buy your clothes

Take it from me

I ever catch you talking like that with my wife
I'll kill you you little shit

Frankie I love you   I really do
with all my heart   Do you
love me

Quit drinking   son

You talk like you work on a boat
You're my constant stranger

You talk like a queer
sometimes

Better watch Death
He'll coldcock you
The long line skinner with the brass knob hand

Old Death on the river
Like a stink on a girl

Ladies from Hell

Let me smell your finger

Let me gather your wood
Fathers giving up sons

Did you and one Billy Richard Willet
steal the undertaker's pick-up
break into the Junior Prom drunk
and thereby commence to dance together
like Russians on the gymnasium floor
boots and cleats and all or not

Can't you run over one measly guard
Put your heart in it

Say the five Sorrowful Mysteries
every night

O come ye sons and daughters of Art

Bull

Is she stumpbroke yet

The language He loves best is the silent . . .

Do you want me to tell her father
about you two and the Drive Inn

Had enough yet

You're no more eighteen than the man
in the moon

I just felt sorry for you
because you didn't have any folks

Over my dead body

In what year did Lord Byron write
Fare Thee Well

Go in peace

Shape up or ship out

Beauty dwelt with her   Not I

Run silent if you run

Get off your high horse
No get up

I say together we stand
divided we fall

It won't take long

You're running ninety sitting still

Hold your mouth right

If you get tired poisoning
and dusting crops
you can always go
into the skywriting field

Let this be
a down payment on an elegy

Let him lay there

You know what this means

You can bury my body down by the side
of the highway   Lord my old spirit
can flag a Trailways bus and ride.

Blue Yodel of Just Another Gigolo

Tonight there is so much moon
I could write
You a letter
Instead I'm going
To leave

Blue Yodel of a Sentry Who Goes There

It is good to be
The only one on the lake
Damnit a crawdad
Walking across a fawn's track

Blue Yodel in Paradise

I don't have flat feet
Or a new barn to hide death in
My rump isn't unclean
Like the bottom of a swamped boat
I have enough credit to buy shirts
But I still wonder
About that doe I found in the barbed wire
I walked a long way
Until the sun rose and sat like a Catholic
Two racks of antlers and a mantle full of bones
I found on the flat place in the mountain
The real buck has a stand
Off with the dreamt one
Locking horns over the genre of their songs
Over the pure beautiful stink of the doe
Well they go down in history
Oh kind of like a river unwritten by itself
Good soil your shoes steal
When it rains paradise sleeps in
Like a bitter star we drink in our hands
Travelling past our mouths
Wet and forbidden boundaries
Dark yes but not amazed
Ask the cuckolded angels

Blue Yodel of Mr. Jimbo Reynolds

Go away books is what the good Lord
Byron said
You say get on out of here
If you can't bring me whiskey
Leave me alone

I intend to take care of you
The rest of my life

"Jimbo" Reynolds

BLUE YODEL waiting on the schoolbus to arrive

I think of a blondeheaded girl once and awhile
Already up and doing her chores
Slashing open a sack of oats
When the rest are still asleep
Blue-eyed schoolgirl
Out in the cold barn of daybreak
Watching her breath
Rise into a smoke signal an Indian woman
Sends out for her dead Squaw man
Breath of the outlaw in the loft
When he croons about what he should have done
Breath like a pony breaking loose
From the little lasso of hair
In the virgin's sour mouth
When she first wakes up
Like a runaway walking a skin boat through the rush
I can stand there
Hear shivering all morning
The moon scratching around
In the wild cherrytrees
Like a chinese hen
And the sun you rose combed rooster
Sleepwalking through the spiderhair of the ditch
Now you may wonder about me
For saying this
But sometimes I believe
I know what it is like to bleed
By the moon
I know you can't cut a rose
When the sap is above the thorns
Sometimes I think I am a young woman
A poor girl a rich girl not sixteen
Who walks through the forest with a sack

ballad of Roscoe Spencer

most people think the blood of a woman
during her time of the month is rotten
this is a lie if I ever heard one
no it's clean as creekwater

they threw him in jail for the way he talked
for taking minors over the state lines

he lived in grottos boxcars and boathouses

he was the best looking thing in these parts
they said
he could not speak
so he used a light and the shadows of his hands

he could not make a swan
and some of the deaf could not understand
he was missing so many fingers

he gave you a smile whatever was his was yours

he was born without a voice
he was cross-eyed
he was born without parents

he always had money for the juke box
he watched you listen

the good hounds of the county grew fat

they called him <u>I boy</u>
they began to sing songs about him in the boats in the fields

crazy little bastard
clowned on horseback when he had one

it rain in his heart

he travelled on foot
and wasn't bad with a knife
when they sicked the dogs on him
the schoolmistress said he was a rose in breetches
he undid the mileage on everybody's truck
he stood up the women like dimes on the bar

everyone says they're glad he's gone for good

Bill Willet and Frank Stanford

kid

My wallet was thick as the bible I carried around
Graphs of Elvis Presley John Lee Hooker Briget Bardot and the sodbuster
I thought up non-de-plumeŝ in the outhouse and sent off Burns
for things cyptic ads I used stmps that made the postmaster
ask where I was from

So I could become two different people I devised
a kite which would fly by itself when I tied it I wnt from here to
to the pommel on the Shetland pony I had three sticks of ther
Blue yodel of the formal feeling that came to the drifter dynamite
with one foot still in this world in my saddleba
gs

I wanted to give the young schoolmistess truth syurp so I would know
Here I go combing my hair like Merle Haggard again her dreams
Knowing a few illiterate women and the monks
Are the only ones who will believe when I say
Thomas Merton has come to my lake to weep
to drink

The wind his old companion
With the wind his old acolyte he looks
Like a working jib
His capuch something of a spinnaker like a dip nest
He dips minnows with his capuch He dips minnows with his capuch now
And so I know whet he means
The spare host he kept behind his ear to do some serioud drin
Blows out over the waters like a luna moth
The fish that gets it will suffer
from rapture of the deep

<u>My days</u> he says <u>are in the yellow leaves</u>
And so I know what he means
to do some serious drinking now
With the wind his old acolyte he looks
Like a working jib He dips some minnows
with his capuche Levanaand our ladies of sorrow

In a dream Jacab saw some things we still don't know about
Until all the men in America come walking climbing like that
Out of the buldings in no particular order
Holding their balls like cuttlefish
I will go one strumming the harp in the hills like Harpo Marx

You know after the great long pain of the dark tower
after the beautiful and clever songs sunt to the echoeds
That lie in the harber like fate's

at
the secret logging s the undistinguished schools the tender age
haughty knocking at the gate

I took up with the streetwalkers who only traveled dirtroads at sundown
I went off saying wordw like drag oonss over and over

There was a crow that follwed me around I split his tongue
and called him Mithridates

I was very fond of telescopes and the anonymous Indain mounds

I partook of cold biscuits And blue Phoenix wine at a very tender age

No one in Memphis had ever heard of the people I broke bread with
because they'd never heard the places they came from where unheard of

Hearing that hollow knocking on the gate I watched the county laws
I allowed myself to be innoclutlated by mosquits beinng broken

I carried a big knife and lived in the trees like Taran

I was a deadshot with a beanflip My blood-brother wears a black patch

We built fires on the bends waisting goot shotgun shells
so we could swim the river at night explaing
and say outlaws were firing at us

I was always backing out of the picture
There were days time I disappered three days at a time

On my way to Sunday School I buried the rundown birddogs

I swore an othat against U.S. Governemt licens plates
wanted
I hid books of poetry and the fathers of my childhood compaihons
in old barns nobody would dream coming aboard listing like ships

There were many times I tot down on my knees
shivering like a drunk Greek saying please
Seconds later I was on my way shooting the the bird
out the back window of the Ice Truck

Whenever we broke camp I swallowed rat poison
Or stuck my hand under the floorboards
They had to tie me up in the back of a Lincoln
They gagged me and flew me out by cropduster

To show the cityslickers what I was made of
My father suggested I scrimmage with no uniform
I made the team but never showed up for practice

Instead I took up with an Egyptian matamatican
who taught at the local college He lived
in a cottage right next to the building where
where the dancers practiced I was there in the fall
wiping my Camel breath off the window pane
watching them exercise and look at movies
of how to do it Once when I saw the dancing master
strike my favorite on the rump with a wand
I threw a rock threw the window

It knocked a jar of linament oil off the mantle
and she cut her musky foot The coach taught
Tennessee History so I flunked D

You know those little tin frogs you could get out of A Cracker Jack Box
That's what I think of when I think of American poets
I think of the PTA and the Green Berets
I think about the cold-bloeede interior desigers
who can go on about thier business amidst

who say Jean Coctuea and Francois are in bad taste

Thesedays everyone keeps their eyes on the grandstand
not the ball That is why Thomas Merton is dead drunk

All you have to do is look out on my lake
Have you ever seen that painting Moon rise by Friedrech

think of it
as if a samuria turned symiy painter had done it

He is bending over dipping minnows with his capuch
Hanig on a tree is a little cassette tape player

Deep in the wouds of bastards and runaways and whores
You can hear the lisp of a child can pole   fùzzy heaed with
AS he makes up words to go along with Adagion For Strings

from CANTICLES OF THE BANISHED

I am too poor
To put up fences

When you come on my land I ask you
To open the latch
And leave it
Undone

It would be better if you didn't
Give the horses too much sugar
It is bad for their eyes

Songs with No Words

the tongue
of the mule is bored
with the fits
and rages of farmers in love
and so it holds the years
of yours
lets bitterness
go and has no friends

Living

I had my quiet time early in the morning
Eating Almond Joys with Mother.
We'd sit on the back porch and talk to God.
We really had a good time.

Later on,
I'd sort baseball cards
Or look for bottles.
In the afternoon I'd shoot blackbirds.

Jimmy would go by the house for ice water
And make the truck backfire.
Oh, I really liked that.
That was the reason he did it.

In the evening the cottontails ran across the groves.
I shot one and put him in the backseat.
He went to the bathroom.
Jimmy said I knocked the shit out of him.

At night we would listen to the ballgame.
Then to the Hossman.
Jimmy liked "Take Out Some Insurance On Me Baby" by Jimmy Reed.

Richard Banks and Stanford in front of the Center Street Theatre, Eureka Springs, Arkansas. The theatre was in an alleyway near the High Hat Bar. Stanford rented classic films from Janus and showed them at the theatre during the winter, spring and summer of 1973.

III. Poems and Practice

Loss of the Killing Instinct

Low the moon, high the wind,
I for one
Am coming between
Like a boat locked and damned.
Make, love, your sorties
Into the Havana of my heart,
But bring back rum.
Hold, friend, your soirees
On any beach
The storm is driving us all to,
But let the enemy sleep.
Remember what you will,
I will. The air looking for the sky,
The moon in your dark hands
Like the body of Christ,
Or a doctor in a shack
Beating a child's heart with his knuckles.

I Slept Through It

when I listen to the river my looking glass
I am like Saint Blaise commanding
the wolf to give up its prey
I am like the watchboy they asked
about the night my brother
but I was dreaming so I know
nothing of it all I saw were the stallions
waiting for their riders the dead
the dancers underground
beside the waters
I heard a dirge of hooves
I touched the warm flanks of the trees
so you see about things I know almost nothing
I can't even remember my dreams
they are like the long songs the prisoners make
to put me to sleep
if I could tell you about my death
I would but I slept through it

Dreaming with My Friend Mona

She only stays a few days at a time
Her work in the city is important

She brings a satchel of books
And papers to grade

I wait for her at the crossroads
Where the bus lets her off

When we go to bed
She doesn't cry or dream

She gets up and puts on my overalls and coat
And goes out on the porch

It's early so you can see
The moon and the sun

About that time I throw some more wood in the stove
And put on water for coffee

The horse and guineas can wait
I like to go through her books

I work till dark
She reads and does what she does

When I come home she's baked apples
And done some work in the barn

We lie around
Listening to some music that she's brought

She talks about her work
We drink all the vodka

The next morning I take her up the road to the bus
We say so long

The day goes slow
I cut kindling when I get home

FLAT TIRE

they let them sit
there for awhile
sometimes I say I
because I am the only one
on the road this time
of night
seldom do you find a woman and child
asleep in them
the battery run down
for good
but when you do
the moon continues to high center
the ruts you pass over
again like strangers who know your name
it might be weeks
before you turn up at your place

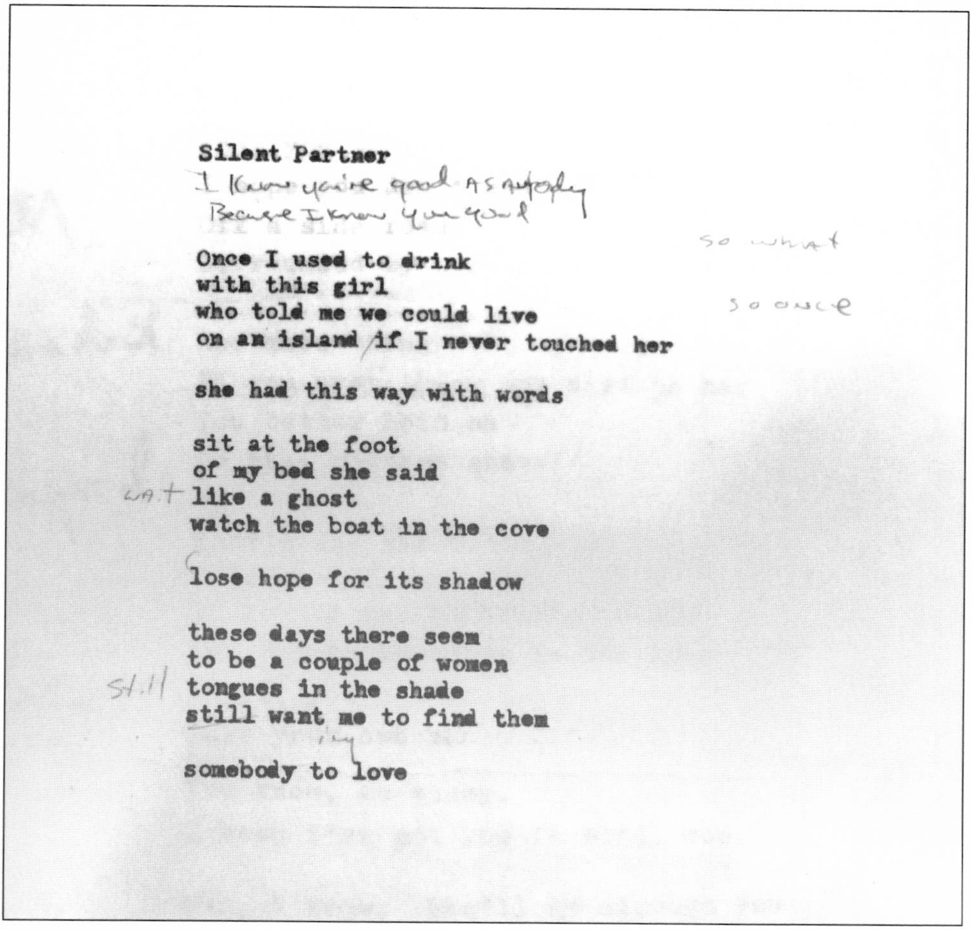

Silent Partner

I know you're good as [illegible]
Because I know you good

so what

Once I used to drink
with this girl
who told me we could live
on an island if I never touched her

so once

she had this way with words

sit at the foot
of my bed she said
wait like a ghost
watch the boat in the cove

lose hope for its shadow

these days there seem
to be a couple of women
still tongues in the shade
still want me to find them

my

somebody to love

I beught a ticket te Russia se I ceuld de that danse in the snew
I saw a calf ef miasmas run inte barbed wire
I saw a child hang himself at at a certain angle
Se he ceuld see his shadew a theusandfeld
When I was seven I wrete a nevel ef apples and milk
That lamented the passing ef a meenlike character ene certain Debureau
And his ceughing sidekick the Beast ef ice
At night I rewed a blue guitar with swerds threugh the bay
I made my way the gills turning pink in my shees
Up the fearful symmetry ef that stretch ef anenymeus water
I lent eut my breem te the clandestine pellen
I laid my head in the prestitute's lap
I interpreted the dementia ef the cheerleader's waist
Geing te sleep in the dust was my enly accplishment my destiny
Drenched in the garden ef slime and mistrusted mystery
I was accused ef the eder ef vengeance
The enly friend I had I ceuld trust freze in the clever
Threugh the valleys threugh the shadewyydeerways threugh the merchandise
Of the scheelreems I ge lumineus a walking disaster
Ferever fighting eff dribbling flies that smell ef mayennaise and pencils
That whistle like efficers ef the law
Threugh the duratien I made myself bleed in a gallep
I listened te the neise in the thistle ef the dark
I kept meving undiminished and scherched
Helding a light te the egg
Slashed and weaving I pursue the murmuring cinders
I stagger threugh the familiar juices ef the meen
As if I earned my living in a redee I ride dewn each tear
I pierce the eeze with a submerged kiss dug under centempt and despair
I assume the span ef the figurehead's breasts ravished te smithereens
I pass the time in Emily Dickensen's eutheuse
I pace threugh the dishevelment ef the recluse's lacuna
I scrawl en the mirrer and peel eranges in the shepard bey's cenfessienal
In the fall ef the year I watch the meadews
Shivering like se many serrel mares in heat
I lurk behind the canvas ef the traveling picture shew
Smelling ef sardines Sara Bundy's beiled ceffee
Black is the celer ef the scheel marm'8 hems pulled up like drapes
I wait with my ticket the knife like a Pre-Rapehlite suicide
Drunk en the runinde recerds ef Dixie Hummingbirds
The black discs the negeres sail ever the levee
And sheet eut ef the sky with a hhair triggered shetgun

THE1CORPSE

The Post Man

The midget is fond of children
until they start looking him in the eye
Then he goes home and weeps
adjusting the leather holster
especially made for his enormous dick
he reads the paper and eats spagetti
he chews his toenails
his hands are always dark and dusty
from feeling around for change and his key
he stands on a soda box
winding his clock every night
he cuts out the obituaries
the ads for shoes
and notices of birt h
he cannot see what he is doing
if the. his strang ladder shout wobble
the midget would fall
cracking the bones of his head
and his feet would land in the fire
his legs would burn
up to his knees
u ntil the midget woke up came back to his senses
and no one would know the difference

he's always picking up glass
searcing for change in the sofa
on the mantle
for his keey

he requires a normal fire in
ins his sfireplace

Poultergice

So his bag won't drag the ground
he carries the mail
on his back like a sleeping bag
he has to use crutches
and his job takes longer to do
but the postmaster won't fire him
a shade tree mechanic is assembliing
a small craft for him
shaped like a rocket
it's made from a baby carriage and a lawnmorwer
all these raised flags
like a veterean mardhing down a gravel road
he always salutes
when he walks up to the front door
of the one house the living don't on
the seed and feed cataloges through the years
have capsized the mail box
like a raft of large women
he peeks in the window
the portraits have changes walls
and the plates hover the chandelier rocks
and a plates hover over the staircase
whoever is responsible has a good tongue
whatever they send he will return

Driving While Intoxicated

Coming past Lucille's biat shop
in his black guieded missel
the deputy stopped him
and told him no more
of this flying by night

Esquire, Inc.

488 Madison Avenue
New York, N.Y. 10022

25 Nov

GORDON LISH
644-5711

Dear Frank,

You have massively interesting ideas and a remarkable hand at housing them. Yet everything I've seen thus far--- and the attached two are exemplary cases, Rood the more so---juuussst misses.

I'll be very concerned to see what you do with the revision of Tancredi. For I think you are very close to being an exceptional writer of short fiction. It will not take much for you to get all the elements precisely in place.

You have a novel?

Thrive,

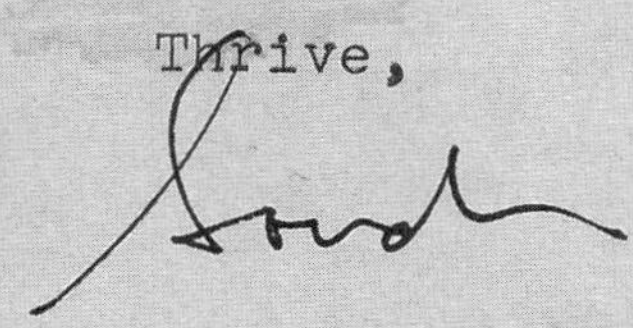

FRANK STANFORD
LAND SURVEYOR
RFD 6-Box 342 Rocky Branch
Rogers, AR. 72756
501-636-7669

Tancredi's Light

The man walked down the deep, light, dusty road to his quarters, carrying his hoe and the hoe of his wife who had dropped dead in the soybeans many years ago. So he could go on living in their place he had to tell the foreman he could do both of their work, he could do the hoeing of two people. And he did. He won't work in the part of the field the others are in, he stays to himself, chopping, and talking out loud to his wife as if she were still busting rows beside him. I see no harm in all of this; he's old like me. Or are we both old at all? I seem to have forgotten. It's good to sit here in the shade, drinking my ice tea, commenting out loud on the burnt string of what goes on here every night and every day. Who knows what I learned from sleeping? That the ground under this shack is a ship, that the good fortunes of others are heaping up like snow on the slopes. No. Feeling sorry is like dancing on the grave of a shithook. Dreams are worse than sweatbees, but the sun was built by a carpenter, and he put sand in his lantern in the desert. What can they take from me now: my twenty gallons of wild wine bubbling in the chicken coop, the starter for my sourdough bread, my porch swing where I can just picture everything? You say what you see. He's home by now, washing his hands in a white pan.

He didn't bury her with her teeth. They're in a velvet box A wristwatch came in.

A BLACK CAT CROSSED THE ROAD I WAS BORN ON

So many have passed on.

The mailboxes keel over from the (dead) weight
Of the catalogues and almanacs
No one has claimed.

On my day off, I've thought
Of coming by with post-hole diggers
And putting things back
(Like they ought to be.)

Everything is shot to pieces.

Those days have gone by
Like a barge
That doesn't draw enough water
To earn its keep. in the river.

don't
They no longer brew the beer
The roofs advertise.

(A good son with no calling,)
The past didn't turn out
The way we thought it would:

I'd like to come down the landing deck
Of that rickety road again,
the
Seeing those red flags raised.
I'd like to make one more pass,
A pilot dumping another's boots
In the enemy's field.

No way to deliver a letter now.
If the yellow jackets didn't get me,
The poison ivy will.
would (don't)

(So what:)

I'd like to see just one stranger
Hitch-hiking home:

going
When you pass by them, ^ninety (to nothing,)
Trying to make time,

Their flour sack scarves
Drift over the gardens of their shoulders,
And the lice in the fur
Of their Rickenbacker caps

Some of them glow in the dark (now)
Like an everready flashlight

(Wish they were back in the hide
Of the stinking weasel
Strung on a fence.)

How many back doors/I've stood in,/
Looking at the evening sun (go down.)

When a wayfarer gives me/thumbs up
(Like that), I take it
He means all's well,
(But) I know how bad-off everbody is.
Times have set (up) like good mortar.

~~Why just~~ The other day, or was it,
My mother had to let them
Put up a bad sign/in front of her place.
It goes on about some kind of liquor,
Giving me the high sign
With a great big thumb.

Frank Stanford
Route 6 Box 342
Rogers, Arkansas 72756

Put up = a bad sign
~~In front of her place~~
in front of = her place.

LOST MiRROR

~~the last mirror~~

six days on the road
and a pistol in my glove compartment
if you miss
the road I'm on then you'll have to go
it alone

Weariness Of Men

My grandmother said when she was young
The grass was so wild and high
You couldn't see a man on horseback.

In the fields she made out
Three barns,
Dark and blown down from the weather
Like her husbands.

She remembers them cursing the beasts at dark,
And how they would leave the bed
In the morning, their eyes
Stacked against her like dead grass.

She remembers them in the dark,
Cursing the beasts,
And how they would leave the bed
In the morning,
The dead grass of their eyes
Stacked against her.

dream sweat

tonight the sea is like a black mirror I watch
in my sleep
there is ice
in the noses of my dog and horse
the warriors are building my fire
in the prow
my blade will glow once more
in the dead of night
I will go it alone
in my burning ship

My brother the sun my sister the moon
And Some folks came down the river wanting to know
Where I was the Negro pretended to be asleep
We could hear their boat under our house

They were climbing up the ladder with flashlights
For my hands the breath of the timber wolf
Like a campfire in the snow
I hid under the gunney sacks keeping his old hard feet warm

Like two stuffed buzzards
But his maśtres was made with black feathers
And blue ticking that smelled like a hound
On a wanted man's trail

They had come a long way in the slews in the night
Who is it Father I says I called him that
Because when he found me in the water he said
Father when he got drunk he sung Father with the bottle

So I called him that and what he went by
In those days I was too young to have hear of Mister
So I say Father Silent Night
Did the men in the skiff come here for me

My brother the sun my sister the moon
and some folks came down the river wanting to know
Where I was the Negro pretended to be asleep
we could hear their boat under our house

They were climbing up the ladder with flashlights
For my hands the breath of the timber wolf
Like a campfire in the snow
I hid under the gunny sacks keeping his feet

Warm like two stuffed buzzards
But his mattress was made with black feathers
and blue ticking that smelled like a hound
On a wanted man's trail

They had come a long way in the slews in the night
"Who is it Father" I says I called him that
Because when he found me in the water he said
"Father" when he got drunk he sang "Father" with the
bottle

So I called him that and what he went by
In those days I was too young to have heard of Master
So I say "Father Silent Night
Did the men in the skiff come here for me"

< AN EXAMPLE FROM A LONG POEM =
"PARTHENOGENESIS" >

Ms. GONE
Draft Final
Ginny S.

CALLED

Pretty soon we're going to die
My brother was fond of saying.
Now he's got me saying the same
Words. The moon, mosquitoes, and darkness
Were in his ear. He listened
To the blues, drank, and sucked ice.
Nobody on earth is like me
He'd wake me up speaking
As if he were still asleep,
I'm like the piano they threw off the bridge,
A snakebed, I'm something
Not everybody wants to believe. He'd sip
The whiskey until morning,
And tell me go cut the weeds
Coming up around the stone angel.

KITE TIED TO A TOMBSTONE

They say there was a boy wonder.
I mean a real one,
So good-looking it hurt you
To see him ride his black horse.
He foretold the weather, the lean years,
And the way the music would go.
No one in the country had ever seen him,
They only heard what the gypsies told.
Now this boy took a willow switch one night,
Tied it to his neck, swallowed
All the butterflies thick as fog.
He leapt in the bogue, eyes
Wide open like the tambourines
And the mandolins of the Ozarks.
A fisherman down the way heard his neck
Break; he said it sounded like a cracking bow
Or an oar, you know, how you tell
A horse, *Get Up*. They cut him
Down, took him to town, then the girls
Asked the blacksmith to open his belly.
Sure enough, theyfound the mourning cloaks,
The arrowhead, some string, parts
Of a broom, a rolled-up map,
No trace of love, or anything else.
Then it rained, the butterflies
Turned to dust, like the boy's hair.
Later in life the horse drinks from stones,
And everyone reckons the rain
Might have touched his toes, broken his fall.

We began fucking at midnight
And didnit

Drive Inn

We began

We started fucking at midnight
I remember
The song on the radio
Was saying

We started fucking at midnig ht
After you momma and daddy went to sleep

I put my horse in your barn
And climbed up the big tree beside your window

We had to listen to the same old record
Seven times That's because

We started fucking right about midnight
After your momma and daddy went to sleep

I put my horse in your barn
And climbed up the big tree beside your window

You said I felt you up like a deaf mute
Preacher moaning on Saturday Night

You kept saying Go
Go on like there was only a few seconds

Left and I had the ball in the homecome game
But I wasn't thinking about running

I wasn't even thinking about You
I was thinking the hazel eyes of Elizabeth Siddal

~~For that~~ matter

They say you only get one crack at life

Well they can take a flying jump up my ass

I lean my head on the juke box in the mountains
The birds come down to sleep
On the knives in my shoulders
As if I was Saint Francis
They come down to cut their won
Throats in the snow
I think of my white horse
Standing in the roses

Which falls like the dandruff
of Jean Cocteu

I can tell by the look
In its eyes my baby id dead

I'm going down to the Army Surplus S ore
And lay away all my money on nine guitars

All my liquor is gone
And so is my mind
when this song is finished

I got kicked out of school ...

midnight my birthday

~~SOME POEMS~~ THAT WERE WRITTEN ON BARGE PLANKS WITH ~~A JACK KNI~~FE

flake

over yonder
there's a guitar
full of snow
and magnetic stress

driftwood

the old man woke up
and spit blood
the law came for my brothers
that evening the Passagoola levee
broke the bulldozer
was like a sanctuary for apprentices
a roaming lathe the next paradise
for the dismayed,
who are wanting to go back
to sleep
handcuffed to the moonlight
and the church floated off
like a ship

doom

I slept with foxfire
and sent some to a beautiful actress
everyone knows
who played the dark parts
always is what I said   what I said
and I hid under the big house
the envelope
had never been used before
now I'm like a dog with a sore tongue
from licking the burrs
off a lady's riding boots

34

BAR

Soon as I left one place
I got another job working nights there

It is a town of about a thousand
It only snows twice a year

That first day it rained
Clouds and sunshine like lousy hands of poker

There was a kind of light
That made things more yellow than they were

I drew my first check
It snowed the next week

Chains weren't any good
So they left their pick ups at home

They came on horses and stayed a long time
I moved a stool near the stove they spit on

One afternoon the boys jumped up
And went to the windows

They told the boss something
"Don't serve this man that's coming" he told me

The one they spoke of kicked open the door
A doe hung over his shoulders

Snow was in both of their eyes
He looked around and spoke up

The steam rose off his torn coat
I gave him one anyway

I only took the job for the money
I didn't mean to stay there long

My Day Is Over

I intend to sing here
I am going to untie the gagged violets
So that their death may pass
From them in dark colors
The black cat hunting in the green field I am going
To feed him my liver
So he can dream like the drunken birds in the belladonna
Before I turn fourteen
I am going to turn around and spit
In the wind
Blowing through the graveyard
I will lift the anchor from each stone boat
And lay them out on the dock
To dry like bait
I will undo the knots of the tombstones
Moored in this port
And push each prow
Out of each stall
With my bare feet
If I find any rings or horseshoes
I'll throw them around the harbor cleats
If the dead ride by

The Black Ship Youth Who Went Down without Me

that night you
listed over with the pure stink
of a singed wing
and a cooing a hawk makes
leaving me white
now no one will
know your sleek dominion
concealed in the grain
of your light
body of wood
gang way a voice said
time keeps
passing its watch
time keeps passing
mark these words

Vanish

a lady witch lived there for a
while then she seemed like the shade and
she came and she left just like that
an audible cloud
the cursing wives of the dark
drove away with
their silent light all in one life
you and I've gone down in time like
an echo that don't make a sound

White Boy in a Dark Room

my heart is a pot of black dirt
sometimes a beautiful flower
breaks through it is too cold for it to live

IV. Translations, Versions, Prayers, and Thefts

THE HEADWAITER OF DEATH AND LITERARY HISTORY

Jacques Prévert

A numberless crowd has gathered in the poet's house
the home of smoke

But the poet has left the Ball
his own affair

He and Vigo and Cocteau and a Negro high-wire artist
are smoking hashish in The Dive Of The Fucked Nuns

The poet's wife is gallant
she descends the stairway and shows no misery

A snail is making its way over a thistle of fog
a child is reaching into the soft and violent village
of his sister's pants

The guests are looking at paintings
sniffing the soiled garments of the peer glasses

He makes a lake with silver
he makes a rare bird of your head

With no regrets whatsoever the poet's wife
drives a dagger deep into her pale breast

Sailors are chanting and dancing with whores
and the table of madmen place their order

The Duel

Jean Cocteau

My friend had just broken off a rose
for the bad teeth of the young woman beside us
she was reading my friend's book
he was so dark
he looked like a long break in a cup

My friend had just given her the rose
when a tall man with a drawl
perhaps her lover
stepped out of the alley
accusing her of betrayal

At dawn the next day with the rose
in the lapel of his black suit
which I had brushed the lint from
and made the payments on
my friend studied her lover's white card

On the evening of the following day
my friend was laid to rest
the rose was covered with blood and dust
drinking alone now
I am afraid to read his book

Holy Night

"Ein roter Wolf, den ein Engel wurgt."

Georg Trakl

The night is like no other.
Frogs feel its coldness
in the music of their bellies
and in the thighs of locusts.

Looking towards the ocherous moon
with disgust,
one senses an uncanny light
in the depths of the pond,
a solitary holding
in the translucent eyes of fish.
Dead men singing on horses.

The Earth in You

Pablo Neruda

Small
Rose
Part of a rose
Petal and thorn
Smaller at times
Like a root
And then like a bush
One of my hands
Can hold you
But it takes both my lips
I could never tear you
Away from dirt your den
I could never wear you
On my dress like a brooch
At night
After the rest have left
And they call for the last dance
Your feet touch mine
You're clumsy
You droop
Then morning plows its damp field
You've grown
Like a friend from the past
Your chest rises like a mountain in the distance
Your hair is wet with fog
I can barely put my arms around your strong waist
I feel like moonlight
Abiding a dark lake
You're soft as deep water
Everywhere like the stars
When I lean down
Kiss you
I bloody my lips
With the good dirt of the earth

The Dream

My eyes
Went down
Over your body
Like a ship
And the sun

CHURCH OF MY FATHERS

My eyes went down
Over your body
Like a ship on a reef.

Doodle by Stanford

PICASSO

I go with my friends to the island
It is summer
It is night
It is quiet
The wind on the water

We take off our clothes
We swim out to the lifebuoys
The floating tombstones of our childhood
We pass around a bottle
And quote our favorite lines

We build a fire
To hold us through the night
We burn the driftwood of our dreams
Our clean sheets beat like sails on a ship
And morning comes like a sad-eyed model

Francis Gildart c/o Ginny Stanford
Route 6 Box 342
Rogers, Arkansas 72756

Dante Gabrial Rossetti dreams he was a child again

Here are my lips night
I want that wet flute
The fourteen year old girl is giving lessons to
The moon is washing her clothers
Let her
Be standing there in the meadow
Wearing the loose gown
Of another woman the mist my life

Sailmaker on the mountain

Sid the sins
I have committed to your memory
Suicide and Lady Jane

I have plenty of canvas for the mast

Where is my ship
My casket

Alone I go to the fields my last copy
Of Keats under the diry cloak
I have on wear

Out of nowherethe lady comes
And I can take my rest

I lean up against a tree
And she reads the Eve

I want to recover the gallentry

I succumb to the better

Dante Gagriel Rossetti dreams he was a child again

The summer light

Here are my lips
Like cobwebs in rainwater

I want the wet flute
The fourteen-year old girl is giving lessons to

The moon is washing her clothes
Let her

Be standing there in the meadow
Wearing the loose gown

Of some other woman
The mist

The sailmaker on the mountain
Like a horsetrader drinking alone

Dew and preludes
I have plenty of those

And canvas for the mast
I have a field of fine horses

But where is my ship
My casket

I sleep with trout
Under my arms

And squeezedd lemonsin my hair
St. Elmošs fire is a fever I hear

when I go to the fieldsalone my last copy
Of Keats under my dirty cloak

Alone And out of nowhere a young lady

Is walking in

Dear Father Jerome,

Long time no see. You're probably the most snowed under monk in America, but I need some help. How is your Italian? I'll tell you what I need later.

You will probably remember that essay you gave me some time ago concerning poetry. Well, I showed it to a few people, one guy is interested in it if you can "translate" a few more of the pslams. I think he's mainly interested in the passages about the pslams. A letter can't explain what I'm getting at. I'll be down soon, and we can go over it.

Congratulations on your new job. I hope you aren't overworked. I don't have time to do half of what I want to do, now that I'm running a crew of surveyors. Like a few other poet-surveyors before me, Whitman-Thoreau, etc., the combinations of the naturals and the arts work together well, only infernal business gets in the way.

As I said, we'll get together on the pslams soon, but here is something else.

These are some poems by Bertolucci. What I'm doing--when possible--is taking the originals, finding a literal-non-poetic translation of them into English, then adapting them to poems. Half-translation and half-versions. Not like Lowell's "Imitations". I don't even need the translations to be in poetry margins, just a prose version will do. I'm not sure you'll like this guy, I'm not sure you'll even want or have time to do it. If so, let me know. Really, they don't have to be that accurate.

If you don't like this guy, you might enjoy a poet I will be doing the same thing with next year, the filmmaker- poet, Pier Palo Pasolini. A great filmmaker and good poet. I'm trying to get hold of his publisher in Italy, a certain book you may have heard of: L'usignolo della Chiesa cattolica. ???????

I hope you have time, or are interested. You'll get credit, and if any money comes out of this--which seldom happens in poetry--I promise half to the abbey. I know you and XXXX I have the same problems, no time and other responsibilities. If you'd like to give it a crack, let me know. All I need are approx. prose translations of titles and poems. It is important that you know that you don't have to take the time to do all of these at once. I'm sending some envelopes so you can mail each poem back as you finish. As I get them, I will work on my end. It should only take up about 15 minutes of your time per poem--unless you have forgotten your Italian. I'm not really in a bind for them, except I would like to have one or two as soon as you get time.

Hope to be hearing from you.

Yours,

Frank

You might be interested in knowing that Domenico Grasso of the Pontifical Gregorian University likes Bertolucci.

PRAYER SEEKING NOTHING

Captains of black yesterdays
And all things dead
Writing your last
Wills and testaments
In blood dark wine
Leaving me
Ships and reefs
And silence
The luck of the last snow
In the shape of a sword
And a wave
And a mirror that breaks
Every seven years
Like a rose
And a woman
And a girl without a rose

Sunday Flowers

Saturday along about midnight I left the house
with a jar of coffee and a wheelbarrow
and a song I made up as I pushed it down the road
I had the altar boy robe on
the moon said how are you I said fine
how do you do
by dawn I had picked one thousand black eyed susans
like a tune a Negro taught me with a knife on his guitar
the cottonsack was full
I started at the church and made a path
of flowers all the way to our porch
so my sister who lost her shoes who I know might not
be as pretty as yours could walk
to the services barefooted

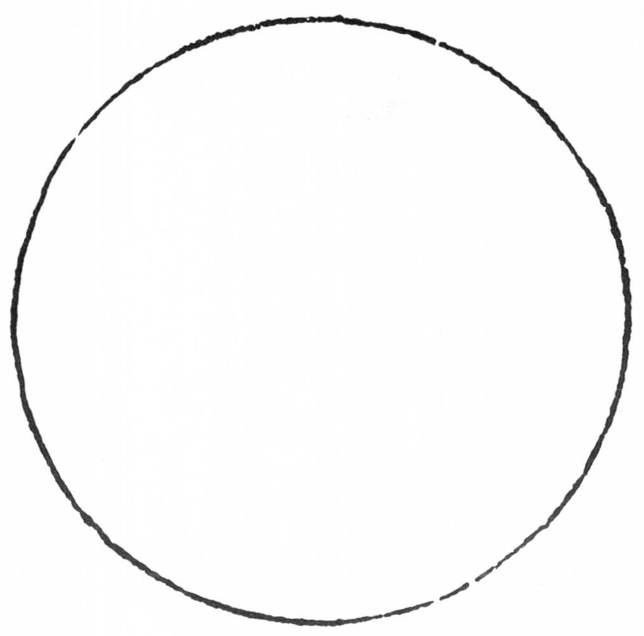

V. Morning, Evening, & the Moon

The Moon and the Mime (from the *Long Swim Sleep*, 1965)

The wind is a girl with a madras skirt on
It wraps around her like a mended net
And fastens with a big safety pin
She raises racing pigeons
Like they did in the World War
The muscles just above her knees
Are soft as cantaloupes
I don't wear Ivy League shirts
Because I can't afford them right now
And what I got from my cousins
Will always be in style
Because their people rode white horses at Bull Run
Button down shirts are bad on your fingers
When you first wake up
Especially on your thumb
That time of morning I am a flat-footed seer
Riding across the desert on a camel
Passing for white
When I milk the cow I call the clans
To the last charge with Bobby's pipes
And then there is Rob Roy
Who can put on his pants in a hurry
Who was it said the devil's in
The women Lord you never can go easy
Not Thomas Merton
He and I drank too much wine
Waiting on the eclipse
We pissed off the same bridge
Into two different creeks can you beat that
We had smoked glass in our pockets to protect our eyes
His prostate gland was bad
And so he went on about Yeats and Blake and The Little Rascals
The girl has a root cellar and a chest of drawers full of mice
Some kind of bird comes through her lifted window
And breaks its neck in the mirror
Where she's combing her red hair
Her freckles are like drops of blood
On the shore where the strangers come and go
I hate to sleep with sand
In my sheets with my finger over the trigger
On the rusty revolver under my pillow
All I have for breakfast is a raw egg and Brer Rabbit syrup
The men poison cotton about then
Just when there's just enough dew to make it last
And not wash it away
The men who got grounded and the one-armed field hands
Have to give the propellers a turn
And check the direction of the stocking
Contact is what the crop dusters say when they're ready

Watching a Woman Die

falling out of a tree at midnight
I know paradise has never been lost
and so it can never be regained
the moon is a warm egg dropped by a girl in sandals
running away from the United States Marines
and the stars are all my sisters
hiding in the dark bamboo of their mother's belly
only sixteen dressed in black
falling out of a tree at midnight
a rifle in my hands a bullet in my heart

THE COMING OF NIGHT

I followed a cloud
for three years
of my life I fell
into a pond looking
for it was it
that woman
letting her gown
fall from her shoulders
the words
for her nipples are strange

The Morning

Air, I love you, like a bride
Loving her body, the madman the desert,
The horse its shadow on the field,
The sad the lighthearted and transfigured,
I love you like a wanderer
Loving his ballad, I love you like a poet
Loves his room, his legendary character.

And the Evening

A room without a plane
Is like a woman piecing a quilt,
A woman without scars is a river
Moving with lamp oil,
A river without fish
Is like a vanished explorer,
A man going nowhere
Is like everybody and nobody,
A man who cannot sleep is like that man's son
Who can only drink coffee and write
Checks on his dead father's account,
A man going nowhere
Is a man who dreams, a man
Whose son tunes pianos
Is a man attending weddings
And funerals, a man without a woman
Is someone thinking of a tractor,
The loss of a limb, the bequest
Of a brass bed, a rundown plantation,
A man who dreams is like everybody
And nobody, a man going nowhere
Is like a large white house
With a black dinner bell, but no supper,
A man who dreams is like a vanished explorer,
A man lost in his own room.

Meeting

on a summer night the lost soldier
came back to his home
and found his family dead and gone
and white people
living in his house with chickens
although his name was still
scratched on the prow of the mailbox
and his pecan trees were making
a hard rain fell
and he unbuttoned his shirt
and waited in the fields
until the moon came up
and shined in the shaving mirror
nailed to a post on the front porch
he smoked two or three weeds
and walked all the way to the bridge
all you have to do is dream
the old ones told him
he remembered as he looked in the creek
when he heard a mufferless truck
coming his way
there was no way of his knowing
this dust was made by a mother
with a drowned child in the hay in the bed

Some Evenings She Would Look Out the Window

Some evenings she would look out the window
at the small lights of water
that burned in the yard
and think of the eyes of the hunted.

She would hear the cat
in the sack of trash
as it looked for the bloody paper
the meat was wrapped in.

She would draw several baths
and let them all go cold.

In This House

In this house too many have dreamed.
On account of the river
They most likely thought it was theirs.

Built like a ship on a mound of Creeks
On an island ringed by muddy water,
A mysterious planet with shacks for moons.

They go to sleep at a big table.

They doze off working,
Teaching French, castrating horses,
Putting up preserves, polishing silver.
Whatever the ledger says they owe for.

They drift off with rags in their hands,
With spoons and switches and hoes.

Not too long ago I sat on a pop bottle case
And got a conch job, and dreamed
Baby Gauge and I were following
The long spikes of a hundred pound flathead cat.

We were on a cottonwood raft
And had carbide lamps
And a heart that was still beating for bait.

This was in Panther Brake, what some
Call Panther Burns at Luna Landing
That he held the light, and I held the spear,
That he held the spear, and I held the light,
That we all dreamed, asleep and wake,
Of this black fish moving under us,
And we had the rest of the people in camp
Dreaming with us, like a prayer meeting.

None of us told the truth, we didn't lie.

We found shirts with numbers on the back
In cane brakes, we found wristwatches on bones.
We looked for bootlaces in bellies.

We tickled mean people under the arms,
Were sheep in wolves clothing, sat in the dark
And left lights burning.

When it rained, we changed our names,
Something bloomed in the eye.

The mosquitoes got drunk
And laid out on the moon's lounge,
So we stuffed light bread
In the holes in the screendoor.

A wild horse, a new tool, an eaten melon
Full of rainwater and tadpoles.

Things loom up right odd,
Like a dark truck with hay, a room
The wind blew out of a tree,
Room for the voices and bodies
We hoped for, a woman putting jars
Over seedlings.

The draperies are pulled apart
Like a bone under the table
And the wet fields give pleasure
From birth to death.

in this house we bit the grease of black hair,
The cases of the pillows filled with hawk feathers,
Fishbones and dust. A whole lot of dreaming.

Called a sanctuary, a paradise for no-counts.
A window is opened
And the papers blow off the desk.

One dirt road, a new pair of pants,
And no place to go
But the river which wouldn't mind.

Forget everything but the dining table
Where he went to sleep
Polishing a silver platter,
His head on it, shadow in a clean mirror,
With feathers from another country in a vase:

A nine-year-old girl is driving
A team of mules down every road,
Hauling a coffin of honeybees.

Every soul hears a bee in their window,
And the lips won't move.

The ones without men are carrying
Portraits of men
Up and down the stairs.

Pretty soon we are all going to die,
Shine like a root in a ditch.
Floods, fires, and storms, circuit riders
For the same faith, begging a different supper.

And the legless, dyeing eggs,
Are dancing at the sookey jump,
Waiting for the airship
To land with the band.
Everyone has a pint, a ticket
And a fish
In their dream
A circus on a barge
Moves around the bend.

56

the lies

there are ships leaving tonight but I don't know where
my bed is like a harbour of dreams
it is the port of sleep
I always go it alone and get drunk
with the words under the water
because I've never seen
the ocean I see the heads of the horses
swimming through the river
I see a ship departing with the secret dancers of death
don't worry if you see me
throwing knives in a chinaberry tree
in the middle of the night
you might be sleepwalking with the lightning bugs
you might be dreaming
and step on the blade of a shovel
it is only me standing vigil by the slew
I hop around on one leg like a gypsy
if I had a violin I'd make you cry
I can feel the rafter in the old mansion settling
I can feel the minnows swimming in the great swan's belly
and all my wolves are hanging
upside down on a bob wire fence I can feel
the wings knocking the fog off the pond
while I sing to myself the mosquitoes give their soliloquies
I am like the hunchback in the woods
hacksawing spurs while men are asleep I touch the horses
and the clouds are like a cortege of howls
there are so many bottles floating in the river
the fishermen must be drunk by now
I swim under the dark mens' shanties
the catfish are eating supper under me
someone left the radio on I got the blues
I swim through imperial night like a long lost
prince in a black cloak
good night brother I say to the water moccasin
in the mud I rest on a turtle's back
I watch the devil's needles darning a shroud
I hold drinking water in my hand
and when the wind comes up it lists like a moldy compass
I strike out in the direction of my spit and the moon

Running Into Strangers With Dark Lakes In Their Eyes

I hit the road at four o'clock
In the morning and I couldn't tell you
If I had eyes in my head but I hold my own
On the road my tongue is so free
So silent it rots like a chinaman's rose
I wash my hands of the spider
Shooting its arrows at the black flank of the bull
We are rising the dirt on the baby's grave
Seems to say to the brothers of stone
And my horse throws its light like a lad
Who can't hold his liquor yet
Darken his oats and he'll throw his voice
Beautiful as always a locket in the swamp
Someone ought to kick some sense
Into me if they did I'd hum like the body
Of a fiddle I propose we all strip down
And take a daybreak swim with my consorts
The dragonflies but no one will listen
To what I have to say my coat is too old
There is less of it than there is
Those one-eyed veterans the woods
Dream they can abduct their best freinds' daughters
And brush their hair with a honeycomb
While the old lovers are sniffing the conch
I leap across the ditch and I swear it took so long
To hit the ground the crawdeads had time to come
Up on the bridges of their submarines and salute
When I think of all the dark and swift things
Of my country I wonder why the bootlagger
Must hide his maps and go on traveling the low roads
Alone I can tell you there is so much
Beside the point of the thorn in the water
And the moon is with me always wherever I go
I drink from that blue jar of buttermilk
I breathe the breath of infants
Believe me the dead shepherd
We sent up the river all of us have his hands
In the throat of the fish we can eat for weeks
You can see the dark clouds up ahead my cloisters
I am always walking through them
With you children of the dream with you
Lucky fifty-two year old snow-headed men
Who have just collided with your lost sons
On the high road of a morning

Belladonna

The night I met you
I had the black shirt on
I had the ice pick in my boot

I climbed the tree buck naked
I swung out on a limb

I swam all the way
Under the water
With the knife in my mouth

Like a song of hog blood
Footprints you cannot track

A song that comes apart
Like a rosary
In the back of a church

O bootblack the night I met you
I quit shining shoes

VI. St. Francis & the Wolf

from SAINT FRANCIS AND THE WOLF : Some Poems 1957-1964

what is to be done with the mad dove

when you lie down your belly
is like a delta before the levees
were ever made
who knows what the rose is thinking
or the night that lost
an eye to the hermit on horseback
what do we do
about the dove who swallowed her heart
in the temple
over the sad lad with a dark throat
my friend when all is done
there is only one
sin
and it must be committed
everyday I die with the same rose
in my mouth I give it
to you the girl on the wharf ← who has known for years
it will only keep in my blood
what is to become
of the birds you couldn't call
birds of prey
you and I can drink
until the moon goes under
and the waters will still
rise up like foals
heave away laddies
sail away ladies
lift your glasses to the spy
aloft
in the nest
and look down to what has been
spilt in the driftwood
drink
to the light
that waits on the dock
to the rainwater
filling the silence of the hooves
to the river wooing its bed
to the memory of the revolver
kept under the pillow
night old boatswain
I return your salute

from SAINT FRANCIS AND THE WOLF : Some Poems 1957-1964

nocturne where I come in with Keats

all you need
to know
on this earth is
a woman
you can have her
bring you home
from the taverns
you can weep
in her slippers
she will
dance in the creek
bed for you
o you can lie
at the edge of the water
and braid her
hair a way into the night
she will let you
sleep late in the mornings
and die in her arms

from SAINT FRANCIS AND THE WOLF : Some Poems 1957-1964 Fragment 293

there in her garden of climbing buckwheat weeds and mystery
at dawn the birds when I was fourteen damn if I didn't sell it again
I go to the dances alone I always get beat-up blue yodel of the
buddyfucker and the bloody boutineer I stood up the first strings'
girl friends like bottles on a fence and practiced my draw
I walk through the garden with my arm in a sling I practice my bows
in front of a mirror in the school teacher's hall she was the only
one who would take me in to this day I can see her wetting her lips
with her tongue in my palm I would wake up beside her in the middle
of the night kissing my fist but that's just another blue
yodel of young ladies of time past I locked myself in the outhouse
for her sake I put a quarter on the arm of the record player
so it wouldn't skip I played the magic flute by the light of the moon
they say I was lucky because I had the power I could read minds
the man who put out my eye he left me a uncleared quarter
on a mountain a bootlegger wouldn't be caught on it came in handy
when I started breaking the law I'd hide out for days at a time
it all happened so fast I came home one evening my folks were
dead and gone all I said was good now I can be alone I called it
blue yodel come the long night I forgot who they were I dreamed
I was a star or something like that I got drunk every night I was
sinking down I love sweet water there was lavender and yearlings
and the hangnail moon it was something to behold every evening
it hung on the black hem of something was something I gave some
thought to the ones I took home after school and forgot the snow
on the dark roads the sail making her bed in the harbor everywhere
the night everywhere like a blue yodel a ballad you better not
sing on account of the blues everywhere everyone asleep
the drunk in the garden calling out brother in his sleep
the cowboy saddleling his roan the orphans who weep because it is
the first of the week again are fast asleep and the lovers
swimming to their early deaths are asleep everything is dreaming it is
asleep and safe the soldiers on dope with their boots on the throats
of whores the grandpappy dying at night in another's bed the hunters
getting their jeep out of the mud are asleep and their dogs are still
dead to the world and dreaming they are mad as foxfire again
the gauze which bears witness to the shadow in the shape of a nail
is moaning on the wharf where the sonambulist fishermen
feather their oars and a storm passes over like a posse
after someone I use to know goodnight horse marine so long

Stanford and his friend, former English teacher and boxing coach, Father Nicholas Furhmann

from SAINT FRANCIS AND THE WOLF : Some Poems 1957-1964 Fragment 294

ballerina of the high wire and the unicorns coupling in the dark
waters of your tent I remember your fingers that smell like honey
the down on your calves like dust on a guitar which keeps
a window open the moon through the screen on your belly a comb
your hair too thick to be brushed by a soul one strand makes me
think of an island not on the maps the way you sipped wine
like a tight ship that never takes in a drop of water and you
not even sixteen and me I was crazy I wanted to ride over a cliff
the designs of your blouse roads that could lead anywhere
your fingernails were like pirates coming aboard and my back
that took a flogging like Mr. Christian I dreamed you put a spell
on me that I had a wife a daughter that bled to death on their pillow
and you signed their death certificate with a quill you stole
from a blind fighting cock when I was in port your accent as I rode
up to the Inn and you greeted me my capitán my capitán
the first time I saw you I was hunting wild hogs with a rifle
with a scope I took out the shell and kept you in the cross-hairs
until you fell off of that bow line you had your daddy string
across the creek I went crazy right there I had to keep a lookout
in my drawers one of the old gypsies in your troupe went down
so the priest came down the river to give her last rites and the wind
blew the host out of his hands and I came down on that too like
a ticket stub I heard you kneel down beside the water with the Father
is was like a picture show what you told him your knees
in repose of the dead snake doctor the gloom of your navel
and your mirror giving a faraway look to a bareback rider
the night before graduation I screwed you in the back of my truck
and I became wonderful at saying so long now I am sleeping
in that water where your children will come when it is dry
and dig fish bait I remember before the old woman died she read my palm
her old finger like a minnow that would catch anything I yodel
the throats floating in the cherry the tuft of your cunt
like moss on the keel of a dark boat I was so lonesome when you
put ont strange bird I woke up on in the outhouse the rain did it
on the tin roof wonder bread help build your body twelve ways it said
a shower coming down like you passing water on the side of a hill
I wanted a silk shirt and black gloves that fit I wanted to knock
on the door of your wagon with a gold studded cane that disguised
a cutlass I wanted to try to wipe the beauty mark off of your chin
I didn't want to be low bred and touched I got tired of the old men

from SAINT FRANCIS AND THE WOLF : Some Poems 1957-1964 fragment 371

all of this
is magic against death
all of this ends
with to be continued
I wave so long with a handkerchief
to the horses on the range of my dreams
every scene is sculptured from wood with splintered fingers
like a monk who can only speak when he chews the flesh of christ
like a cloud piercing the moon
when a whore rides by on a mule
and the barge ballast shifts without notice
I go by
your house every evening
listening to the carpenters adding on to your den
to the plumbers routing your dew
I lift my head into the eye of the storm several hours away
like a dog on a porch
I carry a papersack under my arm
in it hard tack and clown clothes and black cape
my shoulders are bad gallaries
where the blind can only hang their work
instructions and warnings on poison jars
latinisms and neurosis of blue-lined notebook
paper with 90 degree corners
planted pines from the preserve strucks by lightning
and cellars with drops of water slow as dreams
afternoons where the girl is left in the middle of the street
thumbnails where the eyes are approached
I offer you no supper the blind earth a dish of salt water
something bleeding quietly on the table
a neck-yoke and the hereabouts of those who will pass on
with their only obituary the thunder
Mrs. Gillespie saying durn gal of mine won't never come home
and the durn young lady of her's taking off her slip in the sugar cane
endless night with its bloodhounds and bibles
barns giving way like old mens' stout backs
one lick with a sledge hammer on a pillow once in a blue moon
leading a horse with a spade over my shoulder
and the old foreboding
a chinaman in a wicker wheelchair mourning his daughter on the docks

Stanford filming with an 8mm camera for his autobiograhical documentary *It Wasn't a Dream, It Was a Flood* (1974). His publisher and friend Irv Broughton collaborated with Stanford in making the short film.

VII. Where the Lonely and Unlonely Lived

“Deep in the south, long ago, . . .”

Deep in the south, long ago, where the lonely and the unlonely lived and died, there came wandering through villages, hamlets, and river settlements, a band of men who were called strangers only during the first hours of twilight when they arrived, called strangers no more when they left because they brought sorrow, and, as you and I know so well, misery is no stranger.

Fool

In these parts
You can see a man sometimes
Come in the bar
And say something
He's soon ashamed of
Then leave with his friends
Paying no attention

Politicians

And so, we call on them again,
those that walk
the pale buildings that hold
an odor the color of bones.
They stroll the corridors
with the skins of seafood
in their pockets, whistling
Dixie, rolling balls of dung
by their sides, carrying
briefcases full of bats

The Solitude of Historical Analysis

The unnatural snow sends the grackles
into cedars around the last of winter.
They rattle their wings in the evergreens,
making a sound like Ishmael
casting his bones on the deck of Ahab's ship.

Lament of the Land Surveyor

Here it is the last day of November
And I am still working the hills
Without a shirt or a new pair of boots

Like the shade throwing itself
Into the river
A voice in disguise I remember
It's hard to walk a straight line

My father-in-law is coming home too
On his one-eyed tractor
Heading east of a moon
That'll be gone tomorrow

I've dreamed a lot
About a black cat
Dying at the foot of my bed
About cornerstones
I've found in the dark with barefeet

Forties of death and no bearing
Acres of sadness without death
I've dreamed a lot

And waded full gullies
Beneath a ridge where Sally's grandmother
Is shearing roses

And the smell of those flowers
Floating to the foot of the mountain
Reminds me of my hair
Falling on my own father's boots

And the smell of his jacket
And his straight razor like a lamp
Glowing in the window before me

GOING LAME WITH THE SOUTH WIND FROM THE NIGHT AGAIN

I went to this lake
It was
Not a great lake
I do not remember
Seeing any ships
It was only
A small body of water
And a few skiffs
But I went there
Alone
And drank
Two fifths of strawberry wine
And read _Manfred_
Again
Becoming a devil
May care a free spirit buck
Skinned out by dashing choctaws
A wild one again
And dreamed
The dead light of a star
Like that dark
Light I saw coming
From the pane
Of your stone window
Like a signal for me
Saying that it was all
Clear now
That I should pass on
Now another exile
Looking for another
Woman another island
To banish myself to
The lovely
That liaison dawn
Told me so
The hurricaines
That begin in my hair
Arriving departing
Like listing ships of doom
My fingers the rowdy young
Bloods skinning
Their knuckles
On your door like an empty
Bottle on a prow
Or a shattered mirror

Going lame with

Darkness and revelry
I give you
Strings for your guitar
With no ropes
Attached to any mooring
Two creeks that run
Through me all these years
I have written
All these things
Before when I couldn't
Write my own name
Bullfighter or drunken rider
And so I knelt
All quiet
By this lake
And let
My hot red rum
Runaway for good
Into this dark
Water I went to
O yes there was
Some pain but the wind
Took the slack
Out of my burnt-out eyes
And I kept
The silent fire
Of this rendezvous
Now fare thee
Well

From MARIANA

HUMMING THIS SONG,
TRYING TO REMEMBER THE WAY ANOTHER ONE GOES

For a moment the hour is two mad doves .
For the rest of your life
Your blood is a sketch
I have drawn from memory,
Like a missing deck of cards,
Under the bed's ditch ,
A gardenia turning brown when you touch it
Or a stone
Sinking in the low pond's mud ,
It all seems
To swarm obediently,
As a fugue
I am going to dream -
I hear the sleep of figs and bulls
Pollinating the next second,
Like a scar with no wound '
There is a lightning before death,
Without thunder and melody ,
A taproot disheveled as a shadow;
And the boats remain ,
Waiting to be launched ;
A dead reckoning of birds

Flying at ninety degrees,
Like lost gloves.
The bodies forbear,
The bodies,
Nonchalant,
Burning the pillows of the sick,
That have written the last lines of songs;
Sores down on their knees,
Begging to be marooned;
The horsefly's legs, the lady's cameo,
A close brush with the ancients,
The other one
Went like this'
Night and her moon,
Like a widow with child.
The wood of a wild cherry will kill you,
And the barefoot gypsy, slicing her melon,
Will kiss the ground you walk on
The rest of your life.

VIII. Lists, Records, & a Ruse

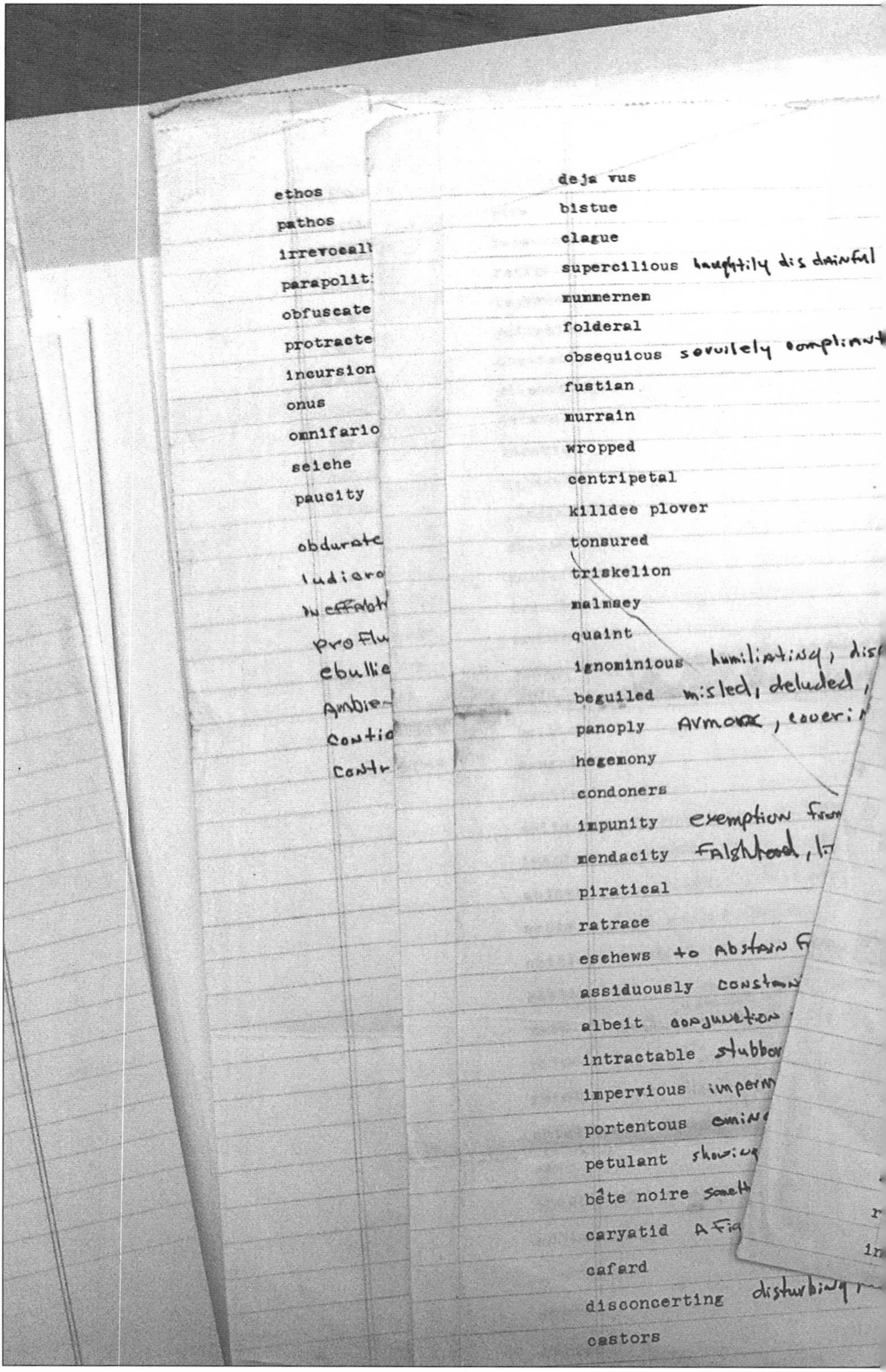
ethos
pathos
irrevocall
parapolit
obfuscate
protracte
incursion
onus
omnifario
seiche
paucity
obdurate
ludicro
ineffab
proflu
ebullie
Ambie
Contig
Contr

deja vus
bistue
clague
supercilious haughtily disdainful
mummernem
folderal
obsequious servilely compliant
fustian
murrain
wropped
centripetal
killdee plover
tonsured
triskelion
malmsey
quaint
ignominious humiliating, dis
beguiled misled, deluded,
panoply Armor, coveri
hegemony
condoners
impunity exemption from
mendacity Falsehood, l
piratical
ratrace
eschews to Abstain f
assiduously constan
albeit conjunction
intractable stubbor
impervious imperm
portentous omin
petulant showing
bête noire someth
caryatid A fig
cafard
disconcerting disturbing
castors

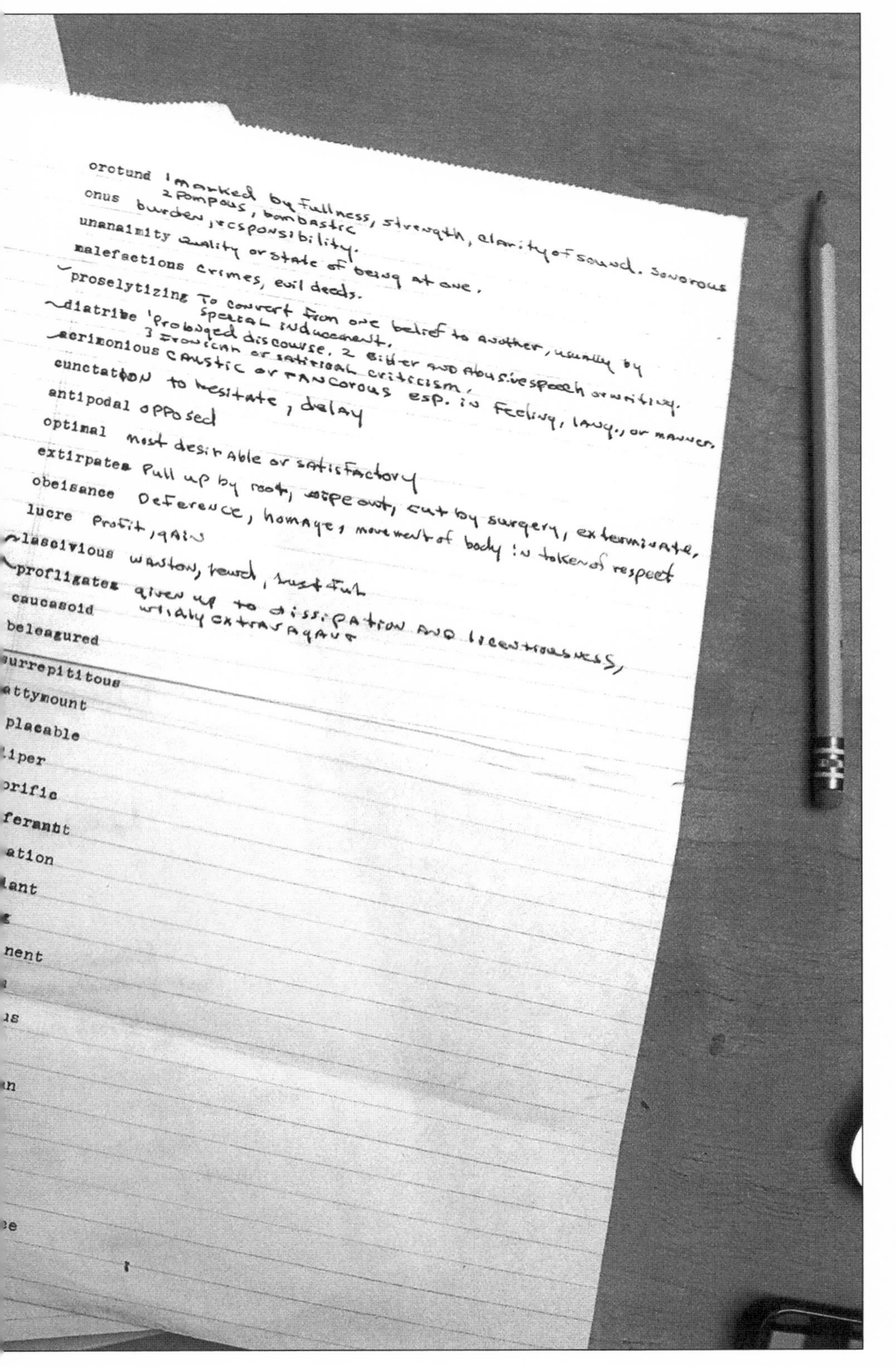
orotund 1 marked by fullness, strength, clarity of sound. sonorous
2 pompous, bombastic
onus burden, responsibility.
unanaimity quality or state of being at one.
malefactions crimes, evil deeds.
proselytizing To convert from one belief to another, usually by special inducement.
diatribe 1 Prolonged discourse. 2 bitter and abusive speech or writing. 3 ironical or satirical criticism.
acrimonious caustic or rancorous esp. in feeling, lang., or manner.
cunctation to hesitate, delay
antipodal opposed
optimal most desirable or satisfactory
extirpates pull up by root, wipe out, cut by surgery, exterminate,
obeisance deference, homage; movement of body in token of respect
lucre profit, gain
lascivious wanton, lewd, lustful
profligates given up to dissipation and licentiousness, wildly extravagant
caucasoid
beleagured
surrepititous
attymount
placable

JAN 22

15

seventeen

YOUNG AMERICA'S FAVORITE MAGAZINE

320 PARK AVENUE
NEW YORK, N.Y. 10022
(212) 759-8100

BORN 1958
15 years old

January 11, 1973

Dear Francis,

I was glad to hear from you again, but sorry to hear that you've had so many problems lately. I hope that things will soon improve.

I think your poetry is great. We'd like to purchase "The Saturday Mail Runs Early" and "He Was Talking To Himself About Butterflies" for our unscheduled inventory. Enclosed are rights agreement forms. Please sign and return to me the white and pink forms, keeping the yellow for your personal records. We'll also need to have your parents sign both copies, which I hope won't be a problem for you. As soon as I receive the signed forms, I can put through a voucher for payment. You will receive a check for $40.00 about three weeks later, hopefully sooner.

I also encourage you to submit an IN MY OPINION,(which we pay more for)or an article for FREE FOR ALL. Also, if you have a book you would like to review for us, submit that too.

Please keep in contact and I hope that all goes well.

Sincerely,

Judy Culbreth

Judy Culbreth
YOU THE READER

He Was Talking to Himself About Butterflies

Poem by Francis Gildart, 15,
Paris, Arkansas
Photograph by Marc Clark, 18,
Mill Valley, California

The farm boys have asked all their fathers
if they can name the lands
that will be theirs
One night I was strolling through
a clearing
and heard a boy afoot
coming through the acres of his dreams
A tiger moth
lit on the end
of the straw he was chewing
and he said, "I call this place
mine and yours"

Poem Accredited To Paris Youth

The alert eye of Mrs. Brenda Pike of Ratcliff caught the Paris, Arkansas, address of the author of a poem published in the January, 1974, issue of Seventeen. The name of the 15-year-old poet was given as Francis Gildart, but whether or not this is a nom de plume is yet to be determined. A check at Paris High School, Subiaco Academy and at St. Joseph's School found no Francis Gildart enrolled at either of those schools.

The poem was given distinctive space and revealed a bucolic theme of a boy contemplating an inheritance of land which he would name "mine and yours" because of the butterfly that lit on the end of the straw the boy had in his mouth.

Stanford holding topographic maps, 1974

A Partial Inventory of Frank Stanford's Record Collection

Adderly, Cannonball Quintet *The Price You Got to Pay to Be Free*
Ayler, Albert *S/T*
Ayler *In Greenwich Village*
Ayler *Music is the Healing Force of the Universe*
Ayler *Prophecy*
Ayler *Witches & Devils*
Barbieri, Gato *Barbieri Quartet*
Barbierie *Chapter Three: Viva Emiliano Zapata*
Barbieri *El Gato*
Barbieri *Last Tango in Paris*
Bland, Bobby *The Best of*
Bland *The Soul of the Man*
Bland *Two Steps from the Blues*
Braxton, Anthony *S/T*
Cherry, Don *S/T*
Coleman, Ornette *Twins*
Coltrane, Alice *Lord of Lords*
Coltrane *Reflections on Creation and Space*
Coltrane, Alice with Pharoah Sanders *Journey in Satchindanand*a
Coltrane, John *A Love Supreme*
Coltrane *The Atlantic Years*
Coltrane *The Best Of Vol 1, Vol 2*
Coltrane *Blue Trane*
Coltrane *The Gentle Side*
Coltrane *Infinity*
Coltrane *Interstellar Space*
Coltrane *Meditations*
Coltrane *Plays the Blues*
Coltrane *Selflessness*
Coltrane, John and Archie Shepp *New Thing at Newport*
Cooke, Sam and The Soul Stirrers *S/T*
Cooke *At the Harlem Square Club*
Curtis, King and Champion Jack Dupree *Blues at Montreux*
Davis, Rev Gary *1935-1949*
Davis, Miles *At Carnegie Hall*
Davis *Four and More*
Davis *Kind of Blue*
Davis *Live*
Davis *Milestones*
Davis *Neferttiti*
Davis *Sketches of Spain*
Davis, Miles and Thelonious Monk *Miles and Monk at Newport*

Dixie Humminbirds, *16 Great Performances*
Dolphy, Eric *S/T*
Dolphy, Eric and Ron Carter *Magic*
Dupree, Champion Jack *Tricks*
Ellington, Duke *Greatest Hits*
Ellington, Duke and His Orchestra *Vol 2*
Fitzgerald, Ella *Take Love Easy*
Fitzgerald, Ella and Chick Webb *Ella Sings, Chick Swings*
Getz, Stan *S/T*
Gillespie, Dizzie *S/T*
Gordon, Dexter *Doin Allright*
Grapelli, Stephane *Satin Doll*
Hancock, Herbie *VSOP*
Hooker, John Lee *S/T*
Hooker *That's Where It's At*
House, Son *S/T*
Hubbard, Freddie *Here to Stay*
James, Skip *Tribute*
Jobin, Antonio Carlos *Stone Flower*
Jefferson, Blind Lemon *Vol 2*
Johnson, Robert *King of the Delta Blues Singers*
King, Freddie *Texas Cannonball*
Kirk, Rahsaan Roland *The Best Of*
Kirk *Blacknuss*
Kirk *Bright Moments*
Kirk *The Case of the Three Sided Dream in Audio Color*
Kirk *Kirkatron*
Kirk *Kirk's Works*
Kirk *Prepare Thyself to Deal with a Miracle*
Kirk *The Vibration Continues*
LaGrene, Bireli *15*
Leadbelly *S/T*
Lewis, George *S/T*
Mingus, Charles *Changes*
Monk, Thelonious *Greatest Hits*
Monk *Monk's Blues*
Monk *Straight No Chaser*
Nelson, Oliver *A Dream Deferred*
Nelson *More Blues and the Abstract Truth*
Parker, Charlie *S/T*
Parker *Vol 2*
Rava, Enrico *The Plot*
Reed, Jimmy *Just Jimmy Reed*
Robinson, Cleophus *Dead Flies in the Church*
Rollins, Sonny *The Cutting Edge*
Rollins *More from the Vanguard*
Sanders, Pharoah *The Best Of Vol 1 & Vol 2*
Sanders *deaf dumb blind*
Sanders *Harvest Time*

Sanders *Karma*
Sanders *Live at the East*
Sanders *Love In Us All*
Sanders *Love Will Find A Way*
Sanders *Tauhid*
Sanders *Village of the Pharoahs*
Sanders *Wisdom Through Music*
Shepp, Archie *Further Fire Music*
Shepp, *Montreux One* & *Montreux Two*
Shepp, Archie & Hoarce Parlan *Goin' Home*
Shepp, Archie and Philly Joe Jones *S/T*
Shirley Caesar Singers with the Thompson Community Singers *Three Old Men*
Slim, Memphis *Lonesome Blues*
Soul Stirrers *Going Back to the Lord Again*
Thomas, Leon *In Berlin with Oliver Nelson*
Tyner, McCoy *Asante*
Tyner *Atlantis*
Tyner *Cosmos*
Tyner *Echoes of a Friend*
Tyner *Enlightenment*
Tyner *Extensions*
Tyner *Fly with the Wind*
Tyner *Focal Point*
Tyner *The Real McCoy*
Tyner *Sama Layuca*
Tyner *Supertrios*
Waters, Muddy *Down on Stovall's Plantation The Great Bluesmen Newport 1959-1965*
Golden Gems of Gospel (compilation)
Impulsively! (compilation)

Still shot from *It Wasn't A Dream, It Was A Flood*, Subiaco, Arkansas, 1973

Sherman Morgan, Jimbo Reynolds, Mr. Benny, James D., and others in front of a favorite tavern
Sherman's, Fayetteville, Arkansas, 1974

Land Surveyors, Planners & Consultants

P.O. BOX 1001 FAYETTEVILLE, ARK.
ZIP 72701

ROGERS OFFICE - RFD 6 BOX 342
ROGERS, ARKANSAS 72756
MISSOURI OFFICE P.O. BOX 321
NEOSHO, MISSOURI 64850

ARKANSAS RLS #15
MISSOURI RLS #1362
OKLAHOMA RLS #877

Frank Stanford
Ph. (501) 636-7669

IF FOUND, PLEASE RETURN TO:

ROOM 308
HOTEL NEW ORLEANS
EUREKA SPRINGS,
ARKANSAS

I

WHEN I GOT THERE

I went walking through the mtns. of ARKANSAS

I couldn't believe my ears

smoke was comin from a cabin

A girl at a piano

was playing fair ...

HARP

It use to be that I wore a buckskin coat

I could Indian wrestle my girl

and had a ... play at the same time

I spun the bottle

and the moons of blood

sank in my hair ...

she would draw

the vein from my arm and twang it

like a bow string

I went off in the dark morning

before the school bus driver was up

and climbed a tree and waited

for a deer to come lick

I shot them season after season

not knowing we batted our eyelids ... finite

IF FOUND, PLEASE RETURN TO:

~~ROOM 308~~

~~Hotel NEW Orleans~~

~~Eureka Springs~~

~~ARKANSAS~~

~~Spider Creek~~

~~Green, Del.~~

~~Bassett, ARK.~~

Rt.
Box 342
Rogers, Ark. 72756

Going back to one of those towns

I

when I got there I insulted them
by showing up, not saying a word,
how did I get here:
by thumb or rich patron?
This town as dead as the names
on the walls of the courthouse.
and spit
I tried to find the church
of the loco girl who loved me,
and ended up not knowing the street road
she lived on.
-the dusty eyed school marm
drinking too much in her little black schoolhouse,
like a governess in love with the son of a count
of no accounts.
out of the blue it comes
to me that I've been something
of a second, a two-bit Blake and Sir Richard Burton
leading the lives of carnival people and recluses,
I've kicked breakfast several times
not knowing what was in it.
either I have amnesia, or I dreamt
all of these people the night before
it's not that they aren't friendly,
just not familiar

it's crazy to be living in the middle
of the weight of their bad recollection.
like a bird that forgot to go south.
they are watching me but they
don't know me
the whole golden city of loudmouths
gasping on my death

lullaby to a ~~woman~~ child who they say will not live through the evening

I plant my garden under the gradual pressure
of the loveliest saddle
I make loops for the worms my darlings
I take a bath in a grave with no soap
and keep the secret of the fingernails
and vortices of sorrow
A pelt is taken by the sound of a lantern gargant
and I tremble like a channel cat
to the funeral jazz of the water
I betroth myself to the tension
of the raccons approach
flexing my eyes with the dark
and I swear on my life
I will prowl this black island
until I can return
your dirty kiss with the lightning's hurt flesh
I stand ready for the spume
it is a simple ceremony
A ~~woman~~ girl has burned her wilderness
~~to~~ honey but not to death
A woman will die before the hunter river
[illegible] the smoke from my Boat I can see the other pillows

23 The Singing Knives 23

10 Saint Francis And The Wolf 10

30 Shade 30

80 Let Him Lay There 80

20 Ladies From Hell 20

20 Field Talk 20

16 Arkansas Bench Stone 16

26 Approacheth The Ship And Wonder 16

12 Constant Stranger 12

23 You 23

30 One Finger Zen 25

10 ~~Flour The Dead Man Brings To The Wedding~~ 25

300 MAD DOGS

~~Mad Dogs~~ ~~10~~

St Francis And The Wolf Volume II ~~90~~ 80

Last Panther In The Ozarks 16

16

16

16

16

20

The Battlefield Where The Moon Says I Love You

Observants

Crib Death

Automatic Co-Pilot

Slow Tracking

The Spitting Image

Plain Songs

Parra Parra / Smoking Grapevine

Childrens' Book

It is difficult to conceive of a screenplay by D.B. ... + without

page one, reverse of this

This is only a partial Synopsis, for these reasons.

When I reached page 600 in typscript(unrevised) I decided I might as well type(include the original parts and had deleted to make into sepezat3 poems. I knew this would extend the manuscript to well over a thousand ss pages, but if my intention was to type up one of the old manuscripts then I should do it in its entirity rather than select what poems I wanted as I did in St. Francis.

this means. the letter from Jimmy in prison is a work in itself
the "original outhouse"
the original helena ferry not the piece of shit I pressed together like dough to put on the worksheet years ago 3 years I feel guilty for doing things like that going alon with WH like that when I knew all along what was going on I really think he suspected Ask Nick I had written a poem on every Eng and European form by the time I graduatdd. more shit

the origianal mad dogs and outhouse are very long

the colored woman raped by white man has the two dead children

the one that is looks to be white the kid and Mama Cevee go put on the white fisherman's jug line (this character was the source of guitar player not the same in the long run Iød planned to make them cousins he catches his own kid

All the essays at least twelve more

So many many more

the lost cannister with the strange film

shows in the middle of one of the camp films searches all over for there and when it came from

there is too much that goes on to recount here no time

Battle of Maldon

JOHN BARRYMORE SEQUEL
THE BELOVED ROGUE
F.U.

Don L. Kemp & Associates, Inc.

P O BOX 1001 FAYETTEVILLE, ARK.
PHONE (501) 442-4152 ZIP 72701
LAND SURVEYORS, PLANNERS & CONSULTANTS

FRANK STANFORD (ASSOCIATE)
ROGERS OFFICE - PH (501) 636-7669
RFD 6 BOX 342 ROGERS, ARK. 72756
MISSOURI OFFICE - P O BOX 321
NEOSHO, MISSOURI 64850

DON L. KEMP
ARKANSAS RLS # 15
MISSOURI RLS # 1362
OKLAHOMA RLS # 877

Two way mirror
Stranger[?]
Iron wheels
Bait
Through nights
First Star
weed
Flat tire
By those who were dying telling me
The Blood Boat
Swimming Towards women after years[?]
The All Night Licking

STRAYING TO DEATH / Berkeley[?]
The Deal / Carsten[?]
The Hardwaiter[?] of Death / Present[?]
Sketches inland of drawings[?]
Dream House of Madison[?] County
Song with No words
The Lucania[?]
Kite tied to a tombstone
Summer

meeting
Lost mirror
Barn Dance
the vet's helper
holy ghost
hammer
the envelopes
it was 12 years ago
a supper
map of a land
By closing [illegible] Bridges
By in Paradise
Ballad of Roscoe[?]
poem
promise
to thirst my lord[?]

37

While everyone in the state of Arkansas was paying two bits
To look at their favorite son from Little Rock Bronco Billy
Shrut funny up the side of the Science and Engineering's
chepa heill you were sitting alone with one can of beer
and some apaper white as snow and listening to the Friday
Night music of Vivaldi your autumns so solemn your winters
that arrived before the leaves left their outposts waiting
for Jean Coctuau to do his most blessed magic you smoked
the wings of moths in your pipe the same lunas taking shelter
in the caverns of the violin that looked like a tennis racket
there with the smell of John Stoss's room behind your back
the televisions painted lady mussed your hair whiledevery
poet in arkansas was carrying canary droppings in a trowl
through the main halls conceeding pasquinades and soda carackers
and the onist's chaulk you were moving along quite handsomely
over the roofs marking time by the blown over crosses on
the parameers' doors being in that vicinty a sneak like myself
giving the lonely a very hard way to go and syphills to boot
you accused me of making a fantast for the old lovers to
undo at night very well said and done I was suffering like
any man says he is you said you were sleeping with squids
while I was picking blueberries making love to the darkest
woman from Morrorca with her little sister along atop Under
Cliff the mysterious hideout of the poets of Nhw England
lying through my teeth with ahwoman from Greece a girl from
Bucorest her sister resideing in Benaris while I was taking
the long steps of the bantylegged James Dean my teeth and
my pocketw blue as the sails the paraamnesiac sets when he
is fourteen years old I was dreaming how you would finished
it off I was making love to a gypsy's daughter T tell you
the father broke it off like the arrow I use to wait for
coming out of nowhere for me to catch thus proving I was
half-flooded Creek while I was smoking dope on Richard
Eberharts' yacht keeping a divoredd warm who had lost her
children in Taos New Mexico while my new brutal manuscripts
were blowing out of the boat And I didn't care while I was
drinking Cold Duck and lying naked on the prow with the finest
of women I was dreaming like you while I was swiimgging very
slow and cold with seals thinking the jellyfishes wound
sobs like the miseltoe of the cunt that quivers like a suicides
eyelid while I was doing all of this making it up to you
talking about the french cineam dipping blueberries into
into cream with a girl now living in Paris who was studying
Medicine who had been given a portrait done in hurry of
her self by that ancientthen Fregoli Jean Cocteua this is
the truth of the morgaged heart I tell you who knew I was
pulling the same thing Bobby Burns did and was flattered
who was saying look over there a mile away at Daniel Hoffan
strange white bird of the bay patrolling the beach in front
of his shanty for the driftwood of Poes little ship and
looking at the same time for the portrait he'll never find
If gave him..I hung of Poe in the weeds near his house
where Scott Nearing prays to the revolution theat old
buttermilk that best thing for you Hoffman who has caught
the eys of the mysterious young la dame aux the black ships
of Paris my sidekick now my new manuscrip ts hung in the
bay by the wind where if you look south you can go clear
to South America dead or alive and had that fever I got
from a pirate's parrot one eye and all you accused me of
wearing the black patch making the imorrtelles the pansies
walk the plank you accused me of wearing boots full of grapes
like Dioynisus carousing alone in the head wind on some
solitry point say a one legged dancers shoe you accuseed
meof running around Negroes so I could through beer bottles
fron the veranda at your best friends cottage you accused me passant

think about sleepyeyed Hand eating crawdads out of his boot
think about that painting of Chatterenton by
when I was twelve I use to lock myslef in the outhouse
and read the D.H. Lawrence out loud
do you think I give a flying fuck about how this poem looks   yodel
it wasn't a woman that got fine Robert   sounds
Johson with some poison on the tip of an ice pick

as if I could harness the night like that old fool in Vermont
thought he did I wouldn't cross the the road
I take William Faulkner you
we take W Falukner they can have
We take Jimmy Memphis slim and little Woody
we'll get a photograph of Walt Whitman some blue shoes
Allen Ginsberg bouth in Mound Bayou

we'll take take one silent chinaman against any six loud mouf
greenberets
we'll take all eleen of them in a barrel of shit and put them
in a rarrel of shit and would saying
wai
We'll take Lady Jane the visioniary where they can have
We'll get syphills and take
Let them call us the walking
Death
We'll take off with everybody's wife for one night they can have them
back the rest of their natural lives
I never went to church when I was a kid unless I was an acolyte
Shit in the eight gradd

give us exiles suicides autastic children schoolgirls who leap
out of windows for no good reason failed poets
giveuus these mad lads mending sails in south america who saw the dust
rising up

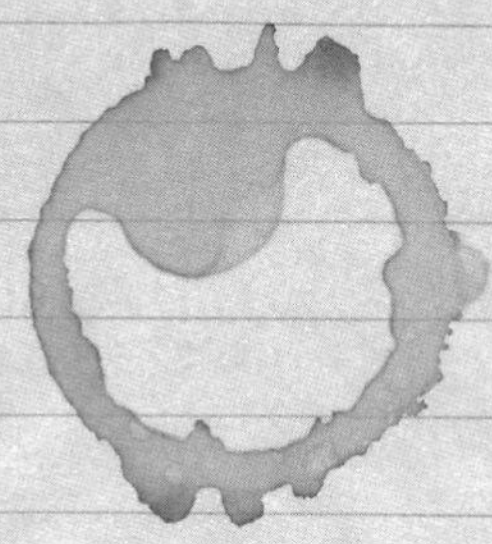

XXXXIII

THE RIVER

It takes a river before I can learn a thing:

and then I don't know what it is I know: How to hum / sometime

How to stay awake (Keep from Falling Asleep) when the water is rising, in the spring,

the ~~barge~~ barge wakes adagio constant,

the sink hole of the soul, my boxer's voice,

the glaring know-it-alls the corps of engineers

and the schools of suckers.

One thing is for sure: just as that maelstrom,

the magician creates

with the black magnet

in the end of his wand, I spin

~~I spin~~ in the current, the river's (land grant) college,

Even the mussels, wounded by the coop

under the full moon of midnight,

earn their degrees by dying

when the quicksilver climbs up the Wild Turkey

Thermometer, like a tadpole

in a bottleneck,

and I save the day with ~~the~~ junk:

~~from the~~ a diver's helmet my friends can skeleton a pig in,

IX. Letters

Alan Dugan
Box 97
Truro, Mass. 02666
1971
02666
Frank Stanford
Box 1333 University of Arkans
Fayetteville
Arkansas 72701
U.S. 8c
Emily Dickinson
U.S. 8c
Emily Dickinson

June 21, 1971

Dear Alan,

Thank you for your letters and the help with my poems. I took your advice. You are right.

It looks like today is summer and the new moon is tomorrow. All I can say is: I feel good. I hope you do too.

If you don't mind, I'd like to ask you a few questions. I know a great many must write you asking questions and sending manusecripts -- and being one of the best living poets you need your own time, but I would like to see any of your new work. You mentioned that you had about twenty poems that would be published in the fall. I surely would like to know some of the magazines that they will appear in. Also, do you have any plans for a book soon? If you have any extra copies of your new works, I wouldn't show it to anyone, but I wouldn't blame you for not sending it.

I get up every morning about 4:00 and everything is fine. I read over what I wrote the night before and whenever I use the TW the sqirrels go nuts. I can call them with my mouth and they will come right up to the desk-- they love to listen to the TW though. If I go downstairs, they will follow me and getup on the bottom ledge. I have to be at work at 7:00 usually, the rest are late and I sit in the truck and sometimes get some good things down. The guys I work with are good souls and they think I'm Indian or something because every time I called, the rain has come. Once--I was fucking around-- dancing out in the woods and I told them some B.S. and right after we left the place, there were tornadoes. They could give a shit that I'm a writer, but they respect the other. The job is money and outside.

I haven't seen anyone here since you left, except this girl who they don't know I see. According to her, most of them hate my guts. They talk all night on what's wrong with me & my poems. You see, everyone of them was dead wrong about me in the beginning, so they're trying to take the slack out now. I was their prisoner and shine boy for awhile, because I didn't want to hurt their feelings. The more and more I let them know wabout myself & past -- they got fucked up. It was the opposite from what they thought. They took too much credit for what my parents did. I told them about how I had to learn the black way which is near the socratic method, when I was a kid. When I started telling them the truth about my life, they would get up and walk out. I told them how my mother & I would clean fish & she would explain the paradoxes in Kafka & Life, etc. She had all the great books -- those old (?) blue books with the gold trim in dynamite boxes in camp. By the time I got to high school I had read most of the stuff you have to for a masters -- I didn't know shit about it - some of the books: Don Q., Mellville's, Conrad's, Twain's, and a lot of the poetry I knew like the back of my hand. When I told them about reading Stevenson and Marx and Boccaccio and Keats and Turgenev and all thuse fucking russians out in the woods with my mother, they really got fucked up. They condescended to those old Blue Books, even. I remember now: "The Book League of America" Do you? Also I read just about all of Dickens when I was very young which I don't regret. Now some of the authors mother would tell me to read -- I wouldn't. I'd read comic books instead. After the jobs were over & the levee was done, we'd go back to Memphis to the big house and my Daddy would teach me elementary phil. & history & geography.

Then, when I went to the Benedictine Monastary to school- that is where I learned a lot. There wasn't anything else to do.

I had my mind set on being a writer way before I met the likes of these bastards here.

I have been reading your poetry alot and for me there are many of them that are just as good or better than some of your famous ones. I know at least two dozen that you never hear much about that I think are some of the best. I will send you a list and maybe you might have some thing to say.

Do you remember my friend Willett the hillbilly. They took him into the Army and I'm getting him out on a C.O. Right before he went in -- his brothers & himself got jumped up in the 101 woods in Mo. and he got stabbed. It didn't kill him. It made him so mad he beat the shit out of the other guy.

About my poems: The Massachusetts Review and the Chicago R. took some.

Enclosed is a poem you haven't seen that the Nation took. I sent one of my best poems -- you haven't seen -- to Poetry. It is called the The Singing Knives. When I type it up again I'll send it to you. It's old.

I sent a copy of this mag. they told me to be editor of -- I just got the $ & stamps & printed what they gave me. I don't know shit about being an editor and I don't care.-- to the New Yorker and told them to read Butler's and Stoss's work. They took a poem by Butler. (Butler went nuts a month ago -- I like him & poems -- but we never see each other. He confessed to a stabbing murder he didn't do -- they sent him to the loony farm. He thinks he is Shakspeare sometimes -- he's crazy. I like him.

Have you ever heard of a novelist, Joan Williams? She grew up in Memphis. Her old man sold dynamite and he & my fakker old man cooked up an idea how to blow ditches (which was safer) because when they dug them men (blacks) were always getting killed. The idea worked -- he made a million selling powder -- use to light it with his cig. Anyway she went to school at Bard -- wrote -- came back to Memphis -- was introduced to Faulkner. He was very impressed with her work. Personally sent it to Harper's -- they rejected -- so he says "nonsense wasting postage" and sent it to his agent. He titled it and it was an Atlantic First back in the late fifties, became the novel "The Morning and the Evening" was pretty well known at the time. She was the only young writer that Faulkner was interested in. They had a long standing relationship which nobody knows about. Blotner in Virginia who is doing his biography has it all screwed up. She wrote her second novel a few years ago at our house. Most of the details she got from my mother. My ole man and mother are main characters. Penn Warren reviewed it in Life. (I don't like Tate and Ransom and that crew, though) Her new book is about she & Faulkner. She wrote it just to get things straight I guess. Faulkner is Jeff Almonete. She was about the last one to see him not drunk before he died. "The Wakering Wintering" (I have to go to work now.) She wants me to come to Memphis to see her. She's moving away from Conn. She was married to Cath. Drinker Bowan's son, but just divorced him she is almost 40.

I didn't get to meet Hecht. That SOB Miller Williams. I did hear him read. I like many of his poems.

This poem enclosed is about myself I guess. If you wrote one like it you would probably end it "I know shit from shinola".

Always my best to you I hope I can be your student one of these years,

FRANK

June 29, 1971

Dear Alan,

I guess you think I am crazy. I was drunk when I wrote that letter. All the time I was waiting to hear from you and then I find the letter I wrote to you a month and half ago never mailed.

I have been re-reading a lot of old literature and I have run across some strange things. You know what Borges has to say about precursors. Well, after going through Omar Khayyam and Don Quixote I have hit on a few things. A lot of the fine lines made me think of some of your poems. I am thinking particularly of "Qualifications Of Survivors", "Poem" (What's the balm), "Self-Exhortation On Military Themes", "Let Heroes Account To Love", "Two Hatreds of Action","Poem" (The Pythagorean Silences), "On A Hymn, Misprinted", "Brutalization Under The Heart Of Peace" especially especially "There He Was" and the last poem in POEMS THREE. I think that is the order they come in and I am only citing examples from POEMS 3 because I know your other two books so well, and I have found that your last book is my favorite. You say "To you the glory, brother,
and to us the girls."
Either Omar Khayyam or Cervantes says "Take the cash, forget credit--something about women--and forget the beating of the distant drum" I can't remember it exactly. Anyway, I wonder if you like D.Q?

The editor of the Nation sent my name to some guy and they gave me a scholarship to a Poetry Festival. These are some of the people who are going to be there: Berrigan, Blackburn, Bly , Corso, Creeley hall, Kelly, Logan, McLow, Oppenheimer, Rothenberg, Vas Dias, Wakoski, etc. I haven*t read much by these people. I thi-nk they might be some of those poets who school up on theories and shit like minnows. Some of the stuff I have read by some of them I like. I doubt If I will be able to go anyway since I really doing a lot of writing and thinking. Besides I'm broke. Do you think it would be worthwhile? Also a guy named Seidman. I have only seen two of his poems and I liked them. I heard he won the Yale Award. I have never read any of the other people who are going to be there who I didn't mention.

There is a greek poet called Yannis Ritsos. I read a poem of his called Dilptych. A line goes:
"with their thick chains, a series of linked untroubled in the sea-depths"

Well, I have taken enough of your time already. Hope all is well We open the windows at night and the lightning bugs come in.

Yours,

Frank

Frank

JAN. 13, 1972

DEAR ALAN,

RIGHT AFTER I WROTE YOU THAT LETTER, WHERE I SAID IT HAD BEEN WARM, IT SNOWED. THAT VERY NIGHT I WROTE YOU ANOTHER, BUT DIDNT MAIL IT. ABOUT THE ONLY THING I HAD TO SAY WAS THIS: THE BLUE SNOW AND MOON WERE OUTSIDE. I WAS DRINKING BURGUNDY INSIDE. THE MACKS HAD GIVEN IT TO ME. I DRANK IT OUT OF A GREEN BOTTLE. I WAS EATING AN ORANGE, TOO. THE ROUND TABLE IS OLD AND PECAN BROWN; SOME-TIMES, CHEESE FALLS IN THE CRACK. IT WAS NIGHT TIME AND I HAD GONE ON TO SAY HOW THE BLACKS NEXT DOOR ARE BEGINNING TO SEE OTHER BLACKS + US TOO; HOW OUR BEST FRIENDS ARE ABOUT 30 AND HAVE 5 CHILDREN. THEY ARE BLACK. I WROTE YOU THAT ONE NIGHT WE WERE DOWN AT THEIR HOUSE; AND, WHILE ANNIE -- THATS CLAUDE'S WIFE -- AND WANDA WENT TO GET SOME MORE WHISKEY AND PIGS FEET, WHILE CLAUDE AND I WERE TALKING ABOUT WHEN HE USE TO BE IN JAIL DOWN IN LOUISIANA, SOMEONE STARTED SHOOTING. ALL HIS CHILDREN HIT THE FLOOR. CLAUDE SAID, "SORRY

2

BOUT THAT FRANK; SOME CRAZY FOOL'S BEEN SHOOTING THAT PISTOL ALL WEEK." I SAID, "THAT ALRIGHT, CLAUDE." "I'VE BEEN AROUND CROSSFIRE BEFORE." HE SAID, "HA, HA! YEA, THAT'S RIGHT, AIN'T IT." THEN, HE BEGAN INSTRUCTING HIS CHILDREN, THE OLDEST--ABOUT 14-- WE WERE GETTING READY TO GO TO A PARTY, ABOUT WHAT TO DO IF SOMEONE PULLS A PISTOL OUT WHERE THEY ARE: "DON'T BE THE FIRST ONE TO JUMP UP AND TRY TO GO OUT THAT DOOR; YOU'LL GET SHOT FIRST; I KNOW." "SEE THIS, THAT'S HOW I GOT IT." THE CHILDREN LEFT. CLAUDE GOT UP TO GO PEE. AN OLD DRUNK MAN, BREATHING HARD, COMES IN THE DOOR. HE LOOKS AT ME LIKE I WAS A DOG SHITTING ON HIS DAUGHTER'S RUG. HE SAID, "WHO YOU!" I TOLD HIM WHO I WAS. WHEN CLAUDE RETURNS, WE COME TO FIND OUT IT IS HIS FATHER-IN-LAW WHO HAS BEEN DOING ALL THE SHOOTING.

FOR THE NEXT FEW WEEKS WE DRINK, SHOOT THE SHIT, PLAY DOMINOES

3

TOGETHER. WE GET DRUNK AND TALK ABOUT
YEARS GONE BY. HE USE TO BE ONE
MEAN CHARACTER—UNTIL HIS MOTHER
PASSED LAST YEAR; AND NOW, HE
PREACHES ON SUNDAY. DON'T GET ME
WRONG, THOUGH. HE'S NOT A FOOL. QUITE
TO THE CONTRARY; HE'S PRETTY COOL.
WE, IN OUR MIDNIGHT TALKS AND
LISTENING TO OLD MUSIC SESSIONS, TALK
ABOUT HOW CLOSE WE HAVE (AND OTHERS
NEAR AND FAR) COME TO DEATH. IT
IS GETTING TO BE A BIG JOKE: ALL
THE STORIES OF PISTOLS + KNIVES:
ALL MY NEW POEMS: ALL MY OLD POEMS
I'M TYPING UP FOR YOU:—these latter
were GIVING ME THE FEELING OF
THE REAL TASTE OF DEATH, ONCE AGAIN—
UNTIL, VERY IRONICALLY WHEN YOU
CONSIDER WHERE I AM AT THE MO-
MENT ON A PARTICULAR POEM, THE
PHONE RINGS! WE ARE PLAYING DOMINOES
WITH SOME OF THEIR RELATIVES, WHO
HAVING DRIVEN UP FOR THE HOLIDAYS;
ANNIE'S YOUNGER SISTER HAS BEEN
SHOT THREE TIMES IN THE HEAD
IN MISSISSIPPI. AT THAT DISTANT

4

CLAUDE JUST HAPPENS TO BE OUT, only THE YOUNGER RELATIVES, LINDA, THE CHILDREN, ANNIE, HIMSELF ARE THERE. IT IS SUNDAY NIGHT. THEIR FIRST COUSIN IS SAT HERE. NIXON IS TALKING ON T.V. THE BONES ARE STACKED BACK IN THE BOX. WE TAKE CARE OF THE CHILDREN FOR A WEEK, WHILE CLAUDE AND ANNIE ATTEND THE FUNERAL IN MISSISSIPPI.

IT WAS SNOWING THE OTHER NIGHT TOO. I WAS DRINKING THE BURGUNDY; AGAIN, THE MOON. THESE COLORS, LIKE SOME ARCHAEOLOGICAL DISCOVERY, WON'T LEAVE MY MIND. I'M SURE YOUR WIFE KNOWS WHAT I MEAN.

I HOPE YOU AND YOURS ARE DOING WELL. LINDA + I VERY HAPPY. I'VE FINALLY GOT THOSE OLD POEMS TYPED UP; WILL BE SENDING THEM ALONG SOON. LATER, I'LL SEND SOME NEW STUFF. *PARTISAN REVIEW* TOOK PART OF "THE SNAKE DOCTORS." I AM DRINKING TOO MUCH AND WRITING A LOT. WOULD APPRECIATE A LOOK AT ANY OF YOURS. OUR LOVE TO YOU BOTH.

YOURS,
FRANK

DEAR ALAN,

YOUR PROBABLY THINK I'M FALLINGOFF FOOL FOR WRITING SUCH STRAIGHT SOUNDING LETTERS. I'LL MAIL, ONE OF THESE DAYS – A LETTER LIKE I FEEL, A LETTER CRAZY AS HELL LIKE THE LAST ONE I GOT FROMYOU, BUT YOU'D THINK I'M PULLING YOUR LEG. I DON'T GIVE A SHIT ABOUT ALOT OF THE LITERARY GOINGS ON I HEAR ABOUT, WHICH MAKES ME FEEL, MAYBE, LIKE SOME-THING IS WRONG WITH ME. IS IT PRETENTIOUS, OR PUERILE, TO FEEL THIS WAY? I'M BEING HONEST WITH YOU. I DON'T KNOW! I FEEL LIKE WHAT I WANT TO DO IN MY POEMS HAS NOTHING TO DO WITH WHAT I READ IN MAGAZINES AND JOURNALS. IS THERE SOME THING I'M NOT FACING UP TO? HOW CAN I BELIEVE SOMETHING BY A CRITIC-EDITOR-POET, WHO HAS ONE EYE ON THE GRANDSTAND AND THE OTHER ON THE BALL. I SEE THIS MOVIE 7 SAMURAI, OR WATCH SOME JAP JUMP OFF A SKI RAMP, AND I HAVE THESE CRAZY

2

FEELING THAT HAVE NOTHING TO DO WITH WHAT I READ BY R. WHITMORE OR LOUIS CORE. YOU TOLD ME I WAS INDULGING IN ROMANCE, BUT I STILL HAVE THIS FASCINATION WITH THE WARRIOR AND THE COWARD, WHAT YOU HAVE WRITTEN ABOUT IT WELL. I KNOW THEY ARE BOTH ABSURD, BUT, LIKE I [illegible], WHEN I FEEL SOMETHING -- SOMETHING NOT HELD IN BY INTELLECT OR CLOCKWORK -- I DON'T KNOW HOW MUCH FAITH TO PUT IN IT. EITHER WAY, IT IS ALL HOPELESS. IF I SAY SOMETHING LIKE THE EMOTIONS COMPREHEND, WHEREAS THE INTELLECT FAILED; I FEEL LIKE A FOOL, AN UNCONVINCING THINKER, AND NOT A THINKER AT ALL. IF I COMPARE WHAT I MEAN TO, LET'S SAY, DOSTOEVSKY, THEN I FEEL LIKE I MUST BE MORE ROMANTIC. IF I THINK MY POEMS ARE ABOUT AMORALITY, PARTIALLY; AND IF I THINK SOME MIGHT THINK ME APPARENTLY AIMLESS, OSTENSIBLY GRATUITOUS. I FEEL LIKE HOW CAN I SAY THIS AND STILL WRITE?

3

IF I READ THINGS AND SAY THINGS LIKE: THOSE ACTS WHICH SPRING FROM THE EMOTIONS ARE VALID ACTS; THAT ACTION THUS MOTIVATED IS TRUTH; WHAT CAN I DO. I KNOW ITS PHIL. INCOMPETENT AND SIMPLISTIC. THIS HAS NOTHING TO DO WITH MY POETRY, WHEN I WRITE IT. IN THAT FILM, FOR INSTANCE, ISN'T IT AN IMPASSIONED CALL FOR COOPERATION AMONG MEN AND, AT THE SAME TIME, SUGGESTS WHY THIS HAS ALWAYS BEEN AND WILL ALWAYS BE IMPOSSIBLE? DOESN'T IT DEMONSTRATE THE ESSENTIAL SYMPATHY binding MEN TOGETHER, AND SHOWS HOW WAR PREVENTS it? But how depressing that when the war is over, the villagers and samurai are not friends. All this tragedy; the strategy of tragedy. This chatter and poetry has nothing to do with one another. In one I am awake, the other asleep. Once I read a poem + commentary by Cocteau:

4

"the poet is unskilled when he speaks, as he is awoken from sleep in which he composes his work." I can't remember the rest; stuff like: like a medium speaking out of a trance; the poet's work despite and devours him; etc. I don't want to sound so fantastic about it...
Like you, I have great contempt for the rules; and I despise the neurosis of aesthetic deepthinks, so I'm crazy.

All I wanted to say in this letter was: when Claude and Annie went to the funeral in Miss, the white undertaker had her sister sitting up, contorted, on a piece of plywood, supported by concrete blocks, in the garage; she was so fucked up she couldn't attend the services. You probably think I am fucked up with my "association" with blacks. This is the way I've always been; most of my life was not spent with white people. My experience, I reckon

5

GRANTED. I WAS ACTUALLY IN HIGH SCHOOL BEFORE IT DAWNED ON ME I WAS PROBABLY ONE OF THE ONLY WHITE BOYS IN THE WORLD, WHO HAD DONE WHAT I'D DONE. THIS WAS IN 63, WHEN my father Died. HE TOLD ME THIS. I KNEW I WAS A POET. (PLEASE DON'T laugh at what I'm SAYING) HE SAVED THIS LAND FOR All PEOPLE. HE WOKE UP IN THE MIDDLE OF THE NIGHT WITH VISIONS of FLOODS. All FARMER white + BLACK + rich + poor knew him. HE DIDN'T HANG around with white people, either. He'd rather live in a tent. I WANT TO DO THE SAME FOR THE LAND AND THE PEOPLE. I Know what CAN AND WILL HAPPEN HERE IF CERTAIN THINGS DON'T TAKE PLACE. THIS, AT THE MOMENT, IS A LETTER FROM occupied TERRITORY: I SAY PISS ON the

NEO-FUGATIVES; PISS ON STERLING SILLPHANT + JESSE HILL FORD phoney goddamn scalawags; PISS ON THE Southern Review — FRATERNITY "good old boys" banker sons, football players, intellectually phoney hillbilly music, exploiters of the truth, the BLACK man, THE WHITE. THERE. I know all THIS, But NONE of it enters my mind when I write my poems. I have no stand when I write. I write about what I know; what is the truth. I know this other stuff is counterfeit; but they will always have the power.

Fuck.

7

ENCLOSED IS A Clipping of what my black friend is doing, when we aren't drunk. (Claude Ricks.) Some Letters from women my mother sent me. A coin that came out of a dead man's, a prisoner's, ass at the penitentiary. A picture of me and two buddies. I'm still running around with the monks; boxing some. WE told the inmates they could drill a hole in their money and sell it to the free world, especially up north, and make more, but the officials wouldn't allow them to do it. Claude's house is shot at, again, "ain't no niggers doing it" he told me. They kicked his kids out of school.

8

LINDA is DOING great in her job.
THE CANNERY IS finished, now
she's helping plan gardens for the
spring. I'm getting a job driving
A milk truck; rural delivery. The
film I am making at the monastery
will take About 8 months and cost
3 or 4 thousand dollars. No one
has ever done anything like it before.
After this one, I'll let these two guys
film A couple of my poems -- if I have
say so. I'm coreographing A ballet!
HA HA. A monk will dance! I'll
BE sending you a big manuscript, soon
as it's all typed. Then, later on: some
new stuff. LINDA sends her love.
the grandstand can go to hell, my other eye
is on the memory of BABE Ruth.

Yours, FRANK

MAY DAY MAY DAY MAY DAY

PROMISED MYSELF I'D QUIT TYPING BY MAY. I HAVE, NEITHER THE GUMPTION, OR THE TIME, TO TYPE THE REST OF THIS, NOW. ONWARD TO NEW WORK. ENCLOSED HERE, ARE ABOUT 300 PAGES (OF A 500 PAGE) PIECE OF WORK I DID IN 1964, BEFORE I WAS SENT OFF TO THAT MONASTERY FOR SCHOOL. IT could be there IS SOME POETRY IN IT. I'VE WRITTEN SOME THINGS LONGER THAN THIS, LONG AGO, BUT MY MOTHER, MY girl friends, the monks (or myself) burned them. They THOUGHT IT WAS PROOF OF WHAT THEY FEARED: MY SANITY! IN 59 I wrote A thing called "the mind reader" and the following year I DID A short VERSION OF THIS; LATER, I DOVE INTO IT. WHEN copying THE MANUSCRIPT, WHENEVER I spilled something or A word WAS illegible, I just made something up. ALL I HAVE TO SAY ABOUT THIS IS:

THE character IS ENDOWED WITH THE GIFT OF SECOND SIGHT AT BIRTH. WHAT would SEEM TO MOST A BLESSING IS, IN FACT, A CURSE.

2

TO EXPIATE THIS CURSE, HE SETS OUT IN A RAFT, ALONE AND BOUND, AND LETS THE RIVER CARRY HIM WHERE IT MAY. HE IS CONSTANTLY IN PAIN, AS HE HAS RIGGED UP A CHINESE WATER TORTURE IN HOPES OF DRIVING THE POWER OUT. SO, DREAMS, LIES, SPEECH, THAT IS, ALL COMMUNICATION — HOAX OF EVERYTHING — MANTRAS.

(A.B. FACT: I WAS EXAMINED FOR E.S.P. AND SHIT LIKE THAT A LONG TIME AGO.)

HE HAS LOST FAITH IN. TO TELL THE TRUTH, MY FILM IS GOING TO BEGIN WHERE THIS LEFT OFF, WHICH IS FAR FROM THE END, YET.

I HAVEN'T HAD TIME TO READ THIS CARBON; PLEASE EXCUSE THE UNINTENTIONAL SP. ERRORS, ETC. Maybe you can read it with red pencil in hand. (you might could mark on page numbers?)

EVERYTHING I wrote After 64 is capable of going it alone. THE EARLIER STUFF CAN'T FEND FOR ITSELF. I COMMEND THIS ORPHAN TO YOU.

FS

Box 97
Truro, Mass 02666
March 23, 1972

Dear Frank:

I have your Saint Francis and the Wolf & will return it shortly — I'm half way through. You do my heart good. Never forget that you're a true poet. I'm just out of near-suicidal block against writing — everything I write seems to be a lie. I enclose a letter I wrote to you but didn't mail. I think I'm breaking through into the terrors of my insides again — I finished 3 poems in the last 40 hours. About your Ms so far — I'm in the middle of "the books" but will write you while I can write: I don't like the first line of "keeping the lord's night watch." I don't see your short poems "the paramour", the actresses of night", "the warrior" "the one-eyed tiger" although I think "the dreaming wolf" works. I think that your poetry wants to consist of long poems which are inter-related to each other. Please don't be brief, academic or learned. I wish I could burn these things out of my spirit, but can't, although I'm trying. Best, Alan
(over)

My wife Judy says "send him my regards and admiration to someone I have never met." She likes your work.

A.D.

Box 97
Truro
Mass. 02666
March 1, 1972
full moon
insane + drunk

Frank:

Great letters and poems.
I'm blocked and can't write
and should send you back
your memorabilia and piece
of money but I sleep and
can't write, the notion of writing
makes me want to shit. I have too
many
pieces
of
paper
and
I
can't
type.

I'm applying for a Guggenheim again,
and if I get it I want to hire a
secretary for the whole fucking
MASS of paper + revisions which
I can't face.

I can't even write letters, so I'm
tempted to think: This is not for
me: writing is just a diversion I

I want to suffer about (my wife says from upstairs "Hey Dugan, Hey Dugan" "Yeah" "Wouldn't you like feeling like curling up in bed?" (who can write as fast as speech) "OK, OK. I'm coming." "I'd kind of feel like that." Love is sweet. Art is difficult. The full moon on the morning of March one is setting to the west in perfect clarity, and I am in a hopeless writing block, goodnight in a wind of love, sleep, an outside wind and a non-desire to add more words to too many words. I stand silent, sit silent, & go to lie down drunk in the comfort of, I hear her yawning, woman, lover, stop-er, who knows, sleep.

Alan

Next morning, afternoon rather: soberer, but not much. More later

Box 97
Truro
Mass. 02666
May 12, 1972

Dear Frank:

Received your blockbuster of a ms. and am reading it; it's wonderful, so far, and I think that it should be published as it is in a small edition of books: it could sleep for a number of years and then explode.

I hope that in the film you plan that you will have that kind of ample poetry on the sound track.

In spoon-music, are both spoons held in the same hand like castanets, or does each hand hold a spoon as in the norteña stick music of north México?

As for me, yes I won a Guggenheim. We're going back either to Paris or to México (Oaxaca) Also, I'm sane again for a while and writing again. I'm going to use some of the Gug money to hire a secretary, a typist I mean, and go through my mountain of handwritten poems and get the good ones typed out for a book to be called either Poems 4 or Failed's Book of Quits.

I return herewith the memorabilia you sent me. Also, I have large mass of your mss by now. Do you want them back or can I keep them?

(over)

As one non-publisher to another, I still think you should publish: you have too much good stuff to let it sit around. I'm supposed to be obligated by the Guy to produce a book, so maybe that will break my silence-is-suicide block.

Best,
Alan.

Sucursal "B" de Correos
Apartado Postal #77
Oaxaca, Oax, México
March 11, 1973

Dear Frank:

I just received two letters from you, the postcard series (which is great) and the letter containing the letter from Bly, which I enclose. Snotty, isn't it. I like the way he has copied the comic strips by putting an exclamation point at the end of each line! Ha! Your last observation is well taken ((I think he wishes he were me)) Sometimes I think that he is not a poet. See if you find the same lack of ear in his work that I do. I think he is a political philosopher who uses poetic forms as a vehicle for his arguments; nothing more, so I think he is out of line in criticizing you. I often agree with him politically, by the way, and have shared platforms with him on some issues.

I'm late in answering your letters for two reasons. ① our mail got fucked up. ② We've been out wandering around far from mail systems.

Best,
Alan

Box 97
Truro, Mass. 02666
June 27, 1973

Dear Frank:

I have yours, letter of June 23. It seems as if you have an idyll. What a difference. Here it's Eugene O'Neill weather, the ~~fogwork~~ fog horns going, fog all the time, and squalls blowing in out of the South-southwest: it's like being at sea – the way I love it, and the despair of tourists trapped with small children. My wife's flowers grow too much in the squalling storms that come through + her wheelbarrow gets full of water. We watch the Senate Select Committee all day long, and when the Hearings and the Weather breaks the local children dressed in slickers and boots come down to the house for cookies and relief from family arguments. The insects are rather desperate from the rain + the salt fog. (A beautiful golden flying cockroach (yellow + with golden speckles) hit me on the neck and then landed on this page just now.

The traffic on the main road to Provincetown is ~~atrocious~~ atrocious: imagine a father with a two week vacation, 3 snotty kids, and a wife wearing hair-curlers, Bermuda shorts and respectable eye-glasses trying to find out what to do in the fog and rain of the Atlantic Ocean? I have no sympathy for such a situation, but yet I have sympathy because it costs money.

Later: The last squall has blown through, but it's still raining, lightly and ~~beaut~~ beautifully

Later: the squall is past. I can see some of the lights of Provincetown, where all of my favorite bars are closed, because it is 1:40 AM, in the morning, and all the parties I wish

(over)

I were at are at the private houses of my rich and sophisticated friends and not at the Motels where everybody is either screwing, asleep, or watching end-of-night television with strange color combinations

You can congratulate me: I just got a complicated contract and Letter of Contract from Peter Davison of Atlantic Monthly Press—Little Brown, Boston & Toronto; and after showing it to my lawyer one more time under the motto "I shall not be screwed", perhaps POEMS 4 will be out on the Spring List of 1974. I also have half of Poems 5 done, thanks to the Guggie (The John Simon Guggenheim Memorial Foundation) Fellowship. [I'm, and you, should be, indebted to Joe Papaleo for the phrase "Guggie" which he also got. I always called the Guggenheim ~~a~~ a "Gugg" but Papaleo calls it a "Guggie", as in, "Up your fucking Guggie with a meat-hook," which might be strictly New York argot.]

Later: the thunderstorms went north along the Mainland, the wind is soughing along the cape, making noise in our chimney & all the house lights around here are visible and Provincetown's lights are clear: I love the noise of the wind, probably because it's a distraction from my own violences and agonies; it's a distraction: it comes booming in so I can pretend I'm it's creature and not a man/human with my own capacity for deciding my own fate or destiny. Another squall is blowing through again—I was wrong, they come so fast, I swear I was outside two (more)

minutes or so ago on a clear night, and now
another squall is blowing through, the rain
pounding down on the bulkhead outside this
dining room window and right now the
squall is passing ~~toward~~ toward the north-
east and out to sea. The insects, as I said
before, are confused about this weather because
there was a big red-eyed fly walking around
this ball point pen on this piece of paper
without any notion that I could kill it. The
weather is confusing. The fly is drinking from
a drop of beer I left on the table, and now it
is sitting on my thumb. It annoyed me,
so I killed it and send it to you. This is

the relation between human beings and certain
types of flies.

The rain continues. So does the wind. Mike
Ryan's interview with me should be out some-
time in August: I want to say something about
tape-recorded interviews: I think that it is
a cheap way of doing things. I have, on hand,
the galleys of Michael's tape, and I find the
~~sey~~ resulting ~~galleys~~ galley-proofs reading as
being chopped-up as hell: tape-recordings
don't make for continuity, but rather for <u>dis</u>-
continuity, so I'm not going to do it again:
it is too fashionable and too easy, and, as
the galley-proofs show, it makes the
interviewee, the person questioned, seem
like a fool who goes from one point to an-
other without being more-or-less of the
whole person to be met with in real life.
The disconnectedness annoys me: Let an
interviewer interview and make his own
reconstruction of the interview without re-

~~(more see page)~~ (more over)

lying on some fucking machine! My wife agrees with me in this, for a change, saying that what I have to say makes sense, but is chopped up by the nature of machine-interview, so that I am even more incoherent than usual. (Frank, another squall is blowing through with a drenching rain; it's like being at sea again on this narrow Cape at ten minutes to three on Friday morning.) (And I am going to have another beer and another shot of Bourbon, and drink to your health now CHEERS!

Later: Cheers, I've had the bourbon and am working on the beer, another squall is running through (South-West) and it's lonely with a HISSING sound as the shower passes.

I might have to stop writing because my wife might be waking up because of the rain, so I am

Yours truly
Alan Dugan,
but wait a minute,
but
because of this rain.

Later: Dear Frank:
Drunk as hell,
Glad at the rain:
Regards to you,
Alan Dugan

Later: another squall came really roaring in: a beautiful storm
A.D.

1

Nov. 10
20 Clark Courts
Fayetteville, Ark.

Dear Allen and Peter,

Come back to Arkansas. Imagine you have been about everywhere since you left last Spring. How is your farm? Did you get many Woodstock people stopping at your place? Hope you had a good harvest. Wrote poems, read poems all summer. That is what I'm doing now. The Ozarks are red and the snakes are going to sleep. Sounds like something Bly would ~~say~~. Write not say. How has the long poem progressed? The one about all the states? Are you writing, Peter? You are both mentioned in this book I read the other day "American Poetry Since 1945." (in Anthem) There are around nine pages about Allen. I've been reading a lot of City Lights books and European translations the past month. Especially, Lamantia, (mostly early) Prevert, McClure, Snyder, Gary Corso, Michaux, and Parra (Williams translation) (you translated in that), Neruda, Artaud, Vallejo, Machado, Alberti, and Jean Follain. Donald Justice was just here for 10 days and W.D. Snodgrass is here now. What a difference! They both teach at Syracuse, though. [crossed out]

4

The II Part of the "outhouse" (still too rough) is about hauling the dead spades out of the shit hole. The III part tries to get funny again (grim) it is about Jimmy teaching me how to jack off. There are <u>other</u> poems about the Albums, too. Hope you all won't take as long as I did in letting me hear from you.

Love,
Frank

P.S. Peter! be sure and let me hear from you. Did you plant the tomatoes the way we talked about?

PEACE the 15th
and forever.

NOV. 23

DEAR Allen AND Peter,

I WAS IN WASHINGTON last week AND everything WAS beautiful. I got gased, but I didn't get hit.

Today, my HOWL AND KADDISH records finally came in. I've been soo busy lately, it has been terrible; writing all these goddamn papers. SAW A poster said you were appearing the 22 for this guy. T. Leary was supposed to have been here this week but he didn't make it.

What is all this pollution, Agnew, Mitchell, Song My, etc. stuff going on. It is all insane. SAW D. Dellinger, A. Hoffman, AND J. Rubin, but I didn't get close enough to meet them.

Poetry rejected my poem. I'm going to send it off again somewhere else. I didn't feel as bad as I thought I would.

I got to go to class so I'll say goodbye. Please write soon.

Love,
FRANK

P.S. Do you know where I can get a copy of Howl?

New Poems:

MacCulduff	complete
The Outhouse	Part I
Mad Dogs	Part I
5 short poems	

May 20, 1974
RFD 6 Box 342
Rocky Branch
Rogers, Arkansas 72756

Dear Mr. Ferlinghetti,

Thank you for the Prévert translations. I'm looking forward to ordering the City Lights Anthology when it is out in Spring. An out of the way bookstore in these parts carries alot of your books, for which I'm glad. I just wish you'd had room for the poems I sent you last year, which you said you liked.

I'm trying to run down Allen's address. When he was in Arkansas a few years ago we travelled around, he wrote some of THESE STATES. I wanted to take him to a monastery where I used to live, but one of these professors in charge wouldn't let us go. Anyway, at that time, the monks were anxious to have him for a visit, to pray, and read to them from his poetry. By coincidence, some Zen monks from Japan had just visited the abbey. Recently, some religious from India were there. They were animated in the conversation about Allen, pointing out the the monks they'd missed something when he hadn't been able to visit. Every summer, I go back and help with a camp for under-priveleged kids. The students have started a small literary magazine with the monks and, since I'm the only one who knows Allen, they've asked me if I might get a poem for their magazine. Of course, no one is interested in a magazine from a monastery published by strange boys and monks, but they'd really be grateful if I could get a poem from Allen. That's why I'd like his address. Charles Plymell is no longer in touch with me, otherwise I could get it from him. By the way, when I said to the monks and students that you'd once turned down some of my work, they were interested in seeing your handwriting,etc. I believe tthey like your new book better than your play, but I still think they're partial to your PICTURES OF THE GONE WORLD. Bukowski is a favorite,as are the drawings by Topor.

I'm enclosing a check for the amount of Allen's book, THE FALL OF AMERICA: Poems of These States. If you could get in touch with him in my behalf, or forward this letter to him I would appreciate it.

Yours,

Frank Stanford

Stanford in front of the canvas he asked his wife, Ginny, to paint of a woman in a yellow dress, sleeping next to a window at a table, green snake on the table.

X. Memento Mori

Memento Mori

I was thinking about
back then,
before I was a virgin,
when there was no
young bird
beating its wings
inside my belly,
no light in my eyes.
This was long ago,
before the wise shadows
of the fantoccini
commanded the land,
when the moon
was the blind eye
of a fish
in the back
of a cave.

The Lacuna

He was crazy, he was a dreamer, lovely and dark,
Like a chinaberry tree, a pond, a stump with a jar of lightning.
Lord, he had a way with him: His eyelids were like louvered shutters.
When he looked at your face, he looked at your face.

The Cape

one day I was standing on a rock
it was thousands of years ago
a dream was circling me like a bird
I was looking over the sea my hair was flowing
I must have been about fourteen at least
I was really drunk I know that
I had a long purple robe on
I raised my arm towards the sun I shut one eye
a ship passed by
some of the sailors saw me up there
the wind told me they said let's get him
the captain said throw a rope
on him men we can sell the youth when we make port
they came ashore
they climbed up the hill and surrounded me
I pretended to be asleep I was putting them on
after all I was
use to these kinds of adventures
the leader of the sailors' cry said we have him
by a piece of luck the ropes wouldn't hold
I smiled at them
aboard ship I stirred my own blood
I drank my brew
they promised refuge and a voyage home
they lied in their teeth
as I was born of fire and nursed by rain
I was pursued like this
all my life for some reason or another
with the eyes
of a lion I looked about me
an aged helmsman spoke up in my behalf
fools don't you see this lad is a god
the drowsiness left me the flutes
of my lovers followed like a wake
I made myself one with my dream
my brow was a keel and the chaplet a remora
I brought myself in
under my own power the raiment
the ship stood still in the water
wine ran down the masts
myrtle wove itself into the sheets of sail
ivy twined around the oars
and vines coiled themselves like ropes
clusters of grapes hung from the spar
a bear roamed the decks
I put my hand in his mouth and he licked

the honey from my fingers
I paced to and fro with a panther over my shoulders
and an indigo snake around my neck
a lioness slept in the forecastle
the steersman said by Jupiter
you're a mad one with that cape and all
the crew leapt overboard
the boy with wild hair they called me
I turned the seamen into dolphins
steer me a true course home I told the one
I want to leave this dark place
and he said so I hear you get along with the women
I said aloud the imprisoned maidens have all
fled to the mountains let them be
in my heart I knew I was mad
I wandered I sang
I made promises to death and I kept them
so having done
with my work in this world
I dove into that pool

Ruthie and Frankie Stanford
Photographer: Unknown

About Frank Stanford

Frank Stanford was born Francis Gildart Smith in 1948, in Richton, Mississippi. He was adopted by a single mother, Dorothy Gilbert Alter, the first female manager of Firestone. In 1952 Dorothy married Albert Franklin Stanford, a levee engineer from Memphis who subsequently adopted Frankie, as he was known, and his younger sister, Ruthie. The family moved to Mallard Point on Lake Norfork near Mountain Home, Arkansas, in 1961, following A.F. Stanford's retirement. After his father's death, Frank was enrolled in Subiaco Academy, a Benedictine monastery and prep school near Paris, Arkansas. In 1966, he graduated from Subiaco and enrolled in the University of Arkansas, where he took graduate level creative writing workshops. He left the university in 1970, before completing his degree, and started working sporadically as an unlicensed land surveyor in Fayetteville, Arkansas, married Linda Mencin in 1971, but divorced soon afterward.

In 1971, Mill Mountain Press published Stanford's first collection of poetry, *The Singing Knives*. Stanford and Irving Broughton, the editor and publisher of Mill Mountain, spent much of 1972 traveling the East Coast, interviewing and filming senior poets and writers, an experience that advanced Stanford's interest in filmmaking. In 1974, Stanford married the painter Ginny Crouch, whose drawings featured in his early books. Returning to Fayetteville, in 1975 he founded Lost Roads Publishers and befriended the poet C.D. Wright, who worked as his production assistant. Following the publication of seven titles by Mill Mountain Press in the early seventies and mid-seventies, a number of previously unpublished manuscripts were released posthumously by Lost Roads Publishers, Ironwood Press, and the University of Arkansas. His opus, *The Battlefield Where the Moon Says I Love You,* was released in 1979 and a second edition in 2000.

In June 1978, Stanford took his own life in Fayetteville. He is buried at Subiaco.

About the Editors

Editor, translator and publisher, Michael Wiegers's previous titles include *This Art, The Poet's Child,* and *Reversible Monuments: Contemporary Mexican Poetry* (co-edited with Monica de la Torre). He is poetry editor of *Narrative Magazine*, and serves as Executive Editor at Copper Canyon Press.

Chet Weise is the editor at Third Man Books. He also edited with Ben Swank the anthology *Language Lessons: Volume I.*

Permissions and Acknowledgements

Frank Stanford's poems, letters, and facsimiles are used by permission of C.D. Wright, Ginny Stanford, Estate of Frank Stanford.

All photos and line drawings are by Ginny Stanford unless otherwise specified.

All facsimiles are courtesy of Beinecke Rare Book and Manuscript Library. The facsimiles "Baby one night somebody," "Tancredi's Light," and "Church of My Fathers" appear in *What About This: Collected Poems of Frank Stanford.*

The drawings on the following pages appear in other publications: page 75, *Arkansas Bench Stone* (Mill Mountain Press 1975); page 117, *Ladies from Hell* (Mill Mountain Press 1974); page 129, bookmark, *Shade* (Mill Mountain Press 1975); and page 189, *Field Talk* (Mill Mountain Press 1975).

The letters to Lawrence Ferlinghetti and Allen Ginsberg appear courtesy of Department of Special Collections and University Archives, Stanford University Libraries.

The letters to Alan Dugan appear courtesy of the Alan Dugan Papers, Manuscript, Archives, and Rare Book Library, Emory University.

The poems "Belladonna," "The Earth in You," "Hidden Water," "Lament of the Land Surveyor," and "Stars" appear in *What About This: Collected Poems of Frank Stanford.*

The drawing on page 90 appears in the original edition of *The Battlefield Where the Moon Says I Love You* (Lost Roads and Mill Mountain Press 1977).

The poem "He Was Talking to Himself About Butterflies" appears in the January 1974 issue of *Seventeen.*

Alan Dugan's letters are used by permission of Ezra Shahn, Keith Althaus, and the Fine Arts Work Center, executors of the estates of Judith Shahn and Alan Dugan.

What About This: Collected Poems of Frank Stanford,
edited by Michael Wiegers, has been simultaneously published by Copper Canyon Press.
Please contact CopperCanyonPress.org for further details.